Regina

v

Vagina

Angela Nangle

REGINA v VAGINA

ISBN:1494492709
ISBN-13:9781494492700

DEDICATION

This book is dedicated to my unholy triumvirate: 'Bed Sheet' (Accountant), 'The Whore Whisperer (Lawyer)' and 'Slide Boi' (Barrister) …with an unconnected walk on part by 'Band Aid' (Another Lawyer).

Not so much the wind beneath my wings, but the sturdy flying buttresses of a disused goldmine.

It is also dedicated to 'Vitriol and Violets' who sadly died (2008) soon after the dénouement of the Tax trial. I do not seek to claim any connection! Date of his birth is undetermined, he may have been approaching 50….but it is difficult to ascertain from which side!!

A further dedication goes to my wonderful friend Sebastian Horsley, who also died (2010) (again, with no connection to my trial) and, in doing so, deprived the world of an inspiring and original free thinker. I was most fortunate to have been touched by his genius and the generosity of spirit in his soul.

DISCLAIMER

The title of this worthy tome WAS going to be: 'The Fourth Suck is for Gordon Brown' (for obvious reasons) but, I realise that there are some dullards who may misconstrue the assertion.

FAVOURITE MUSIC LYRIC

'...And you can stick your nine to five livin' and yer collar and yer tie,
You can stick your moral standards, 'cos they're all DIRTY lie,
You can stick yer golden handshake, and stick yer silly rules,
And all the other SHIT, that they teach the kids in school............   'COS I 'AINT NO FOOL'

A/C D/C: 'Gonna be a Rock and Roll singer'
Vocals: Bonn Scott (R.I.P)

ACKNOWLEDGMENTS

'A friend in need is a pain in the arse. ...'

Thank you all for listening when I needed you, and sodding off when the hermit mode beckoned, but, especially:

1) 'The three voices of reason': Cameron: (no not THAT one), Paul: (Ding Dong), and Harry (Essex Thespian).
2) 'The best friend a woman ever had': Julie Burchill Raven (no fair weather friend is she).
3) 'Hat - Trick Patrick' (who came from behind to score).
4) Finally, my poor (in every sense of the word!) family...who have wintered and summered my ups and downs, (and there have been many).

ABOUT THE AUTHOR

Born in Norfolk and raised as a catholic (now 'lapsed'!), Angela Nangle (Letitcia), having endured the ennui of employment in myriad soul sapping jobs, (including Her Majesty's Inspector of Taxes), decided to take the 'road less travelled.'

As a peripatetic global 'erotic service provider', she finally found her niche.

Angela currently resides in Brighton, and, according to 'The Cheeky Guide to Brighton', is regarded as a: 'well loved woman', icon, celebrity and local hero.

She continues to fight the slings and arrows of outrageous misfortune....!

CONTENTS

WARM UP

I despise British Bank holidays. The streets of Brighton are clogged with sightseeing nuclear families playing Mums and Dads and kids, the restaurants are plagued with moronic screeching children who do not know the meaning of the naughty step, much less the words: 'Shut the f*ck up'. For prostitutes, the steady stream of willing punters dries to a Patagonian vista. Yes, Friday to Tuesday we (sex workers of the nation) are all dressed up and no-one to blow, but, come the end of this madness, they (the likely lads with an erection the size of Florida) are straight out of the traps and queuing up like veterans of Harrod's or Bloomingdale's New Year sales.

You can set your watch by it.

There is one more thing that you can positively bank on :- (like strangely enough, death and Taxes).

And that certainty dear reader is this: HMRC letters demanding money with menaces, or suggesting that one should pop along to the local Tax office for a chat (under caution naturally) ALWAYS, but, ALWAYS thud through the door the day before aforementioned public holidays starts.

This is Fact.

They 'allegedly' have a deal with the Royal Mail (or other service providers) to do this very thing for the obvious reason that the poor miscreant to whom the letter is addressed will have up to 5 days of panic and worry. After that psychological trauma, they (the addressees) are thereafter putty in the hands of the enemy.

This is pretty darn clever actually. Whoever thought it up must have been a prize ocean going tool, and no wonder the British public recoil in horror at the very word (sotto voce): Income Tax.

And lo, it came to pass, this very thing HAPPENED TO ME.........

TIE ME KANGAROO DOWN SPORT

Strangers often stop me in the street and ask: 'Are you an actress'

My traditional quip is: 'Nah, but I HAVE faked a few orgasms in my time.'

I sail on, leaving the questionnaire with a look of bewilderment or amusement, depending on how quickly they get my sense of humour.

How was I to know, soon, anything mildly approaching joy and happiness (let alone a sexual climax) would be almost impossible..........

'Drink two litres of water a day.'

These are words which offer eternal beauty to the vain and desperate (me) in this aesthetically preoccupied world.

These words are the reason why I find my bladder is desperate to reach home after a short trip to the shops, and what bliss it is to put the key in the door and offload several pints of Evian.

Sometimes it is a close call to return to my personal bathroom in time to enjoy relief.

The reason being, I have become public property. I wrote a book called: 'BODY WORSHIP' and I have segued from common or garden 'civilian' to what is deemed to be a Z list celebrity, local hero and instantly recognizable iconic personality. That is what it says in: 'The Cheeky Guide to Brighton' and who am I to argue?

Their words, not mine.

One does not want to let the adoring public down, and therefore a certain amount of pain is endured while sweet natured people accost me in the street and ask: 'How long did it take you to write your book?' or 'How are the sales going?' They were obviously thinking that if a 'Prossie could do it' (write a book), they could have a bash themselves!

Meanwhile my bladder shouts: 'this is your final warning' and the heavy supermarket bags scythe through my sausage like fingers.

The sense of release once I have extricated myself from the madding crowd is enormous.

It is a little like bondage........

I don't know how I overlooked the cracking character, with a 'Tie and Tease' predilection, for inclusion in my book: Body Worship (True Stories of a Sex Goddess).

He (the character) was approx 85 years old (honestly), and therefore since it was at least 20 years ago, I figure he has already died and gone to hog tied heaven.

Horace was his name, and he was a widower. This information is significant, since one of the small pieces of frivolity he enjoyed embarking upon, was PLACING HIS DEAR DEPARTED WIFE'S WEDDING RING ROUND HIS FLACCID MEMBER (he was quite puny)....and then feeling the exquisite pain/pleasure of his tumescence growing.

I met him in a parlous, raggedy, threadbare 'Massage Parlour', where for £15, men received a perfunctory 'massage' with perfumed COOKING OIL (I know, it's gross), followed by an even more dispassionate five knuckle shuffle (naturally for an additional fee).

There was no equipment provided to speak of, and one had to improvise with whatever was to hand. So Horace was tied to the massage bed with old tights and the blindfold was an old knitted bobble hat which I pulled firmly over his eyes and secured with gaffer tape.

One needed a heart of stone not to laugh.

I figured a bit of aural deprivation would ice the cringe cake and whacked an old Sony Walkman into his long hairy lugs. The only tape I had to hand was an A/C D/C heavy rock compilation.

I pressed play, stuck it on maximum volume......AND WENT TO SERVICE OTHER WAITING CUSTOMERS IN ANOTHER ROOM.

I checked on the old duffer from time to time and he would be humming away '....I'm on a highway to hell', and doing the geriatric version of head banging quite happily, with his marriage ring, slowly biting into the flesh of his burgeoning pensioner prick.

He would have been quite content to be there all day, but it caused gridlock in the contra-flow of the grimy emporium....so after an hour or so I would finish him off and send him back to the home for war veterans.

His pleasure, was not borne of the 30 second wank which was swiftly administered due to a punter tail back half way up the street (he was in the 'waiting room'), nor was it because he had sullied and defiled his band of gold with octogenarian seed....it was because he had this delicious build-up of expectation.

Another two characters who DID make it to my worthy tome 'Body Worship', adored the same frisson of tension.

Nick was the dispassionate ex-army officer, who held young ladies in complete THRALL with his bondage prowess. They would willingly allow him to bind their masochist bodies' in myriad positions.....and just abandon them.......for hours!!!!

When you are dangling in the countryside from a tree or hanging from a warehouse rafter, I'm sure the eventual relief of escape is quite overwhelming. The fear, the discomfort, and the control that is relinquished, building up to a veritable tsunami of exquisite release from the danger, and culminating in the arms of the bad boy bondage lover.

What a high!!!!

Conversely, 'Mr G' would hand over control to the LADY from time to time. This phenomenon was extremely common with people in 'high powered' or high profile jobs. An exchange of power is not only the element of helplessness that is bequeathed to the woman, but again the fear of 'oh no (oh yes) what the bloody hell is she going to do me NOW????

Throw in 'poppers', various class 'A's, electrics (and I'm not talking Dixon's or Curry's here chaps), whips, paddles, choker, and sand paper (just to get you thinking) and a dildo the size of The Cape of Good Hope, and NATURALLY it's going to be an almighty explosion of testicle blowing proportions.

Mr. G had the chance to turn the tables occasionally with a mega willing participant called Pru. She also was a 'high flyer' and he would 'deliver' her to various Madams in certain Cities of England. Pru would assent to a blindfold before entering the Madams' building and once inside the apartment, her clothes would be taken from her, and Mr. G would leave!!!!!

'Come back for her in precisely one hour's time' would be his instruction.

She would be firmly shackled to, and bent over a 'horse' (not a REAL one you dozy sods), then she would be gangbanged by willing strangers in an orgiastic free for all.

Her thrill was wondering how far they could debase her, and since she couldn't move or see, the excitement was mounting with each act of defilement, until her bone crushing climax.

HIS thrill was one of a vicarious nature.

These are naturally extremes of the temptations of tie and tease, but probably the most popular, is one where there is visual encouragement.......FOR MEN

We are not talking about pain (apart from the gut wrenching throb of the 'old fella') we are talking: HOW LONG CAN YOU HANG ON WITHOUT WANTING TO MURDER THE BITCH.

It's the ultimate prick tease, you (the men) are lightly bound with the finest fully fashioned seamed stockings, or mink lined leather restraining cuffs which can be clipped to the wall at the top of the bed (works for me), your voluptuous vixen is undulating and fixing you with a desultory stare....she is fully dressed in your favourite 'hard on'- making outfit (pick your fantasy).

She strips slowly and seductively (she has gone for lap dancing lessons)...but she's so far away 'come closer' you cry...but she ignores you and enjoys watching you squirm with pleasure and the discomfort of blue balls.

She then starts to pleasure HERSELF.

'NNNNNOOOOOOOooooooooo' you cry in exasperation.

The more you beg the more SHE enjoys it. This is one sadistic siren.....she makes herself come and licks the enormous black dildo which is swathed in her perfumed juices. She exaggerates her licking, teasing and deep throat technique (though lamentably STILL on the dildo) as a precursor to what is on offer.

She stops for a fag break, and pays no attention to you swearing and practically blubbing like a spoiled sprog.

She wanders off to the other room to teach you a lesson in patience....you comply, you have not choice sunshine!!!

She slowly moves toward you and motions that she is FINALLY going to touch you....but after the most fleeting brush of her hand she pulls away. You will now gladly make a Faustian pact with the Devil himself if you could just imbed your twitching tool into a soft palm, a luscious mouth or indeed a juicy quim.

You are straining so hard on your binds that the flying buttresses which support the walls of your bedroom are in danger of collapsing.

When you finally make contact the sensation is magnified tenfold, you make the sound of a wounded beast.

Anticipation, you just can't beat it!!!!!

BUT, being permanently helpless and without choice is another thing, as I was soon to find out.............

GORDON BROWN, AND HIS SH*TTY BROWN ENVELOPES

It was a day like any other, if indeed there was such a thing in my life. The starting point is either 'coming to' or 'waking up', depending on how much alcohol I have consumed on the previous evening.

I have indeed been guilty of a lapse of memory regarding the previous evening's movements, and when I was once asked by a mate: 'did you work last night' I replied 'well, there's a hundred quid on my bedroom floor and I have sore nether regions, so I guess I MUST have!'

I stagger to my living room and look out to sea.

This view, almost without exception, elicits the comment (made by visitors) 'Great place you have here'

'Yeah' I reply 'Great RENT too'

I have come to take this uninterrupted panoramic vista for granted.

'Another shitty day in paradise' I say to myself.

One and a half hours (I couldn't do it in less) is required for honing and creating something which visually approximates my idea of a SEX GODDESS.

A pride swallowing siege of 'topiary' complete with 3 styles of razor, numerous lotions and potions almost work their bad - girl -magic.

Then I paint by numbers to erect a construction of 'Oh baby, baby' proportions

It's my fault.

I modestly came up with the self-appointed moniker (Sex Goddess), and now, along with the encroaching decrepitude of advancing years I'm saddled with it.

Beauty is an illusion, it's all done with smoke and mirrors with a dexterous sleight of hand. Suspiciously dimmed lamps as homage to Blanche Du Bois (Streetcar named Desire you dullards) help considerably. Constantly drawn drapes with a nod in the direction of Miss Haversham (Great Expectations) do the rest.

'That's about as good as it gets you old git' I muse after battling against (what I consider) my visual disadvantages with the cunning, verve and élan of the She Devil herself.

I wonder if they (the punters) DO look at the mantelpiece when they are stoking/stroking the fire.

I survey the edifice I have created in one of the countless mirrors mounted on the walls of my opulent apartment.

I self-pose the embarrassing question: 'Would you pay £200 for that?'

I can't be subjective....I don't have a turgid dick and I STILL don't know what it is men want.

It would just have to do. 'Stuff 'em if they can't take a joke' I think in defiance.

I get dressed to impress, don a ubiquitous hat and bounce out of the door to grab the day by the throat.

On this day, it so happened, it GRABBED ME.

I spied, with my expertly made up eye, a letter hanging out of my mailbox. It could not have been MORE bills, having just cleared the final demand backlog from Christmas time.

I saw the envelope up close and personal.

The words: INLAND REVENUE ...the kind that demand attention, and are the ultimate dampener to the day.

They are up there in the 'pour a bucket of cold sick over you' type words-----along with: 'nuclear waste', 'terminal cancer' and a sickly: 'I think we need a break.'

If those words were a Penis, nobody would relish touching it....let alone sucking or f*cking it.

A Disney cartoonist would have shown my hair stand on end and the blood drain from my face and shaking body.

FUDDING HELL!!! I don't know why I bothered to open it, for I vaguely sensed what the gist of the missive might be.

I was immediately consoled (trying to find solace in the smallest detail) by the error on the first line.

I was addressed as: MRS.

Their investigative techniques were not THAT sophisticated.

Obviously they did not know me well, for, other than that of the local supermarket, I had never been stupid enough to walk up or down an aisle.

Tempting though it was, to stuff it back in the envelope with the words: 'Not known at this address, try Singapore' (A ruse employed by Errol Flynn) I copped it sweet.

Even though I hadn't read the thing, I kind of assumed they weren't writing to congratulate me on my website lay out or my avowed sexual skills!!

When I did peep again at the 'missive de jour' it was predictable bully boy, authoritarian jargon.

'We have reason to believe' it continued---

'Oh for god's sake', I thought 'how much more reason do you need than a Sex Worker having the temerity to raise her head so far over the media parapet, that the entire City of Brighton is holding onto her ankles'.

Then it got to the risibly predictable: 'Use a sledgehammer to squash a grape' bit. Threatening me (standard flanking deployment apparently) with issuing a warrant for my arrest (eek!), but then laughably (and I'm sure, with therapy I WOULD smile in time) saying that in my case they would like to see me to 'explain' the unexplainable.

Gee that was mighty white of them.

We could sit round and have a cosy chat, just like Blair did with his 'Cash for honours debacle'

A date was set (by them) with the edict that I was to let them know IMMEDIATELY, should I be unable to attend.

A smart arse would have replied: 'Actually, I do not care to attend your gathering since I find I am watching the TV on that particular day....many apologies'.

They enclosed instructions as to how to reach the gates of hell: 'The Local Tax Office' and the numbers of the 'Citizens advice' bureau in my area, for they intimated I would surely (sorely?) be in need of legal advice.

That's like saying: 'we are going to pull your fingernails out, and here is the address where this ritual torture will be performed. DO NOT BE LATE.

As it was nearly Easter, I checked the date, just in case it was a practical joke for April fools. No such luck.

A coward would have immediately run back to the comfort of their abode, emptied the contents of a bottle of bleach down their throat, placed an ASDA/WALMART PLASTIC BAG over the head and waited for sweet asphyxiated death.

The rest of my life was not going to be pretty.

In short, I was doomed.

Instead, I chose to get on with my day, I WAS AN ICON AND A LEGEND OF MY OWN MAKING AND I COULD NOT LET MY PEOPLE DOWN!!!

Yes, I was the object of my own creation, and maybe literally, the author of my demise and all because of my desire to write a book.

Having written it, I was anxious for my wisps of wisdom to reach out and tickle the book reading public of the world.

What Hubris!!

The universe (for me) tilted on a weird axis and off I set.

Lumbering and stumbling, rather that striding along the road, I was to be acquainted with the feeling of making baby steps through the thoughtfully provided excrement which Brighton pavement sweepers and dog owners leave to ensure one slides easily through the day.

A delicious fantasy sprang into my fertile mind.

Knock, Knock**

'Who's there?'

'Letitcia'

'Do I know you?'

'Nope'

'So why are you here?'

'I hereby serve you notice that I am going to take the most satisfying dump of my life....on your doorstep'

'Are you mental, why would you do that you crazy woman?'

"Cos' your Burberry coated, diamante collared, designer clipped, cosseted and spoilt 'Man's best friend' has been doing just that for the last 2 years on MINE, and this (removes trousers and assumes the crouching position).............is PAYBACK'.

I relieved myself of canine crap from the sole of my shoe, but still I kept tripping. This was portentous for the coming days, for so consumed was I with this gigantic cow pat in my life (letter wise), that I simply could not concentrate.

My steps carried me by rote to all things that were familiar. Rather than panic, I rejected the notion of a travel agent with cheap one way 'round the world tickets'.

My first encounter was with James: The editor of Gscene: the biggest Gay Magazine in Brighton and beyond.

The fact that I did not bid my normal non PC welcome of: 'Where do you think you're off to, you big fat hairy woofter' was, I imagine, a dead giveaway.

He had registered my 'drained of all blood and bonhomie' type face.

I handed him the letter. In that moment I decided that I would tell anyone and everyone who cared to listen about my, ahem, 'spot of bother' (and eventually thousands of Brightonians ran the other way when they saw me coming with my interminable tale of woe).

Honesty is the best policy, and in my neighbourhood, if you fart at one end of the street they will be anticipating the follow through by the time you reach the other end.

'What are you going to do?' he (James) asked with obvious concern.

It was my first encounter with a person who would know beyond doubt that I DID have feet of clay. In that moment, I saw I had destroyed the 'style over substance' patina of other peoples' perception. I would have to put a stop to that or my cover would be blown.

I wanted to cry but instead I just said: 'Bang to rights, just a misunderstanding, I'll just have to face whatever is coming to me'.

This temporary tearful aberration was unusual territory for me. I was used to the role of court jester and playing to the gallery. Also the hero worship ('Great achievement in writing a book, when is the NEXT one due') element was undeniably seductive.

Now I had to let them know I was a failure----and would probably be a PENNILESS failure at that.

I bade James a farewell with the words: 'Gotta dash possum, I have an appointment for a 'strap on' fantasy due at 12.30 and I need to buy some

AA batteries!'

My public, private and business persona was getting mighty complicated.
What would my humble father have thought of all this???
Why did I have to write my Auto Biography: Body Worship????

NO REST FOR THE WICKED

On the following day I heard suggestions veering from:

'You could always go back to Australia' -----when I didn't even have enough to buy a second hand car, let alone emigrate.

'Go back home to your Mum' ------as if she didn't have enough troubles of her own.

'Change your name and start again' -----like I could have a bearable life looking permanently over my shoulder.

The most unhelpful but strangely appealing one was:

'Make sure you slit your wrists VERTICALLY.'

Yes everyone was a (bad) joker, as in: 'That's why it's called TAX, short for taxidermist....you're STUFFED!!!'

Or there was a leering: 'I'm SURE you know a friendly Judge' ---wrongly surmising my patrons announced their occupation the minute they entered my 'salon'.

So, I got up and tried/ pretended that the harbinger of imagined doom had not arrived at my door 24hrs previously.

The 90 min ablutions ritual remained, as did the wading through emails on my P.C, with email interlopers from the planet SPAM and, who worried about the size of my obese body, non-responsive clitoris /dick and bank balance.

Emails from Nigeria were given short shrift and nobody learned my mother's maiden name, regardless of the proposed amount of money that would find its way into my bank.

I faced the reality of the Revenue letter from hell with the stance: 'What is the very worst they can do to me?'

I checked on the Web, and compulsory clitoris removal was not listed at www.gov.HMRC.co.uk.

Phew!!! What a result. I even felt happy enough to take a booking for a first time 'Virgin de-flowering'

What a happy Easter it turned out to be.

There was Christ with his resurrection and me snatching victory from the jaws of 'going down, but not out'.

I figured 'you can't let ANY bastard grind you down' and I went into defiance mode.

This 'come on and do your worst' naturally oscillated from day to day, but I would not relinquish a life of hedonism for a crappy envelope, devoid of a stamp, sealed with a bit of Sellotape, potentially demanding an extrapolation of money, and more, with menaces.

I called in the markers of the previous panic ridden day, to see if anyone had come up with the components I needed to deal with this mess.

'You're going to need a very creative accountant' (like you can actually choose different types).

'You need a shit hot Lawyer' (ditto).

'You need a bleedin' Miracle' (agreed).

These were the words of wisdom from most of mates in my 'Manor'

It is a tight knit community, and I could tell by the far a way look in peoples' eye that they already KNEW.

The jungle drums had started beating and people could feel my imagined pain and sense my failure to live up to the hype I had created.

I looked and walked like a beaten cur. I had to restore myself to an over enthusiastic Labrador puppy.

To hell with it, I would just have to try harder. As many mates told me: 'you've dealt with worse than this in your life'

Every one became a comedian:

'They don't serve champers in clink you know'

'You'll be used to the cavity searches though'

'They'll need a van just for your hat boxes'

The Schadenfreude shuffle was in full flow.

Somehow I couldn't find anything funny in one comment.

My chuckle muscle had gone temporarily A.W.O.L with no discernable hope of it ever returning before the next major eclipse of the sun, nor of Charles and Camilla winning 'the most beautiful couple of the year' award. I even tried watching the movie: 'Wayne's World'.

For once, the bit where Garth mimes to 'Foxy Lady' did not raise a smile.

Every person thinks that sex workers are the spawn of the Devil and diseased felons who are flouting the law.

I had to find an organisation with Sympathy for that Devil

I searched for help on the Web.

There was no Ombudsman and no governing body to rush to the defence of a prostitute in a pickle.

'The Prostitutes collective', 'Sex workers of the world', 'Adult entertainers Society' and a clutch of tart like organisations purporting on their Website to help a hooker in need, were annoyingly not fit for purpose.

Were I to have been a disabled Lesbian from Latvia who had been shipped into the UK in a sea container I may have had more luck.

This specialist subject needed a savoir, and they weren't it.

I was behind the lines in enemy territory and needed the troops to bring me home. They left me to rot in the fetid jungle, and didn't even return my 'Mayday' call.

Life is all about learning, and this was a belated truism: There are no

Marines for Masticators of Cock.

The delicious irony of tax payers money being wasted on those organisations purporting to help the 'unfortunates' was not lost on me.

I needed to find my freedom fighters to lead me into what might be the most fearsome battle of my life.

I idly flicked through the labour of love that was my Autobiography.

There, on the very last page, I had (unwittingly) given a literary 'v' sign to my Ex Employer from all those years ago: HER MAJESTY'S INSPECTOR OF TAXES.

Oh yes, if I have to land in the shit, it has to be the biggest, most noxious vat the universe has ever seen.

I actually DID secure employment there, in the days when owning the L.PS' 'Frampton comes alive' (Peter Frampton) and 'Dark side of the moon' (Pink Floyd) was mandatory.

In the closing prologue of my book (which I would use as a speech at the Oscars if ever I was nominated) I wrote these words: 'and to the faceless Tax Officer (higher grade), who at my annual assessment said: 'we are interested in WINNERS here, not LOSERS' the following'...........

Oh yes, I had 'flipped the bird' and invited them to sit and oscillate on my fist.

THIS (for them) WAS GOING TO BE PAYBACK WITH KNOBS ON!!!!!

I had the temerity to 'diss' the most powerful body of poisonous plebs the world has to offer.

I had to laugh, and assumed (wrongly as it happens) they had stumped up the cost of my book as evidence for the prosecution. Who says that crime does not pay!!!!

Their revenge would be sweet. They (I assumed) had the technology and they held all the cards. Game over before it began. After all, 'a Smith and Wesson would beat four aces' as they say.

My mate Kei suggested I get a 'nice little Phillip Treacy hat in the colour of Taupe' for my forthcoming 'interview with the Devil'

'You are going to have to learn to act humble and be submissive' he counselled.

'Believe me,' I spluttered 'I have never been so submissive in my life!!!!'

I was a study of the word 'supine'.

After many false starts, I found just the accountant I was looking for.

How I arrived at the first member of 'Team Letitcia' was a strange set of circumstances that had its origins in an email to my Brighton Body Worship website which I received nearly ONE YEAR previous.

PADDY FIELDS OF PASSION

Yagnash, the local newsagent commented: 'Oi Letitcia, are you sleepwalking?'

Ha, bloody ha.

It was 8.30 ish in the morning----as opposed to the mad 6.59pm 'trying to beat the clock' with regard to getting to my Daily Mail (well SOMEONE has to read it) before they closed.

I had an assignation.........

He was a married man with 2 children. We drank coffee and talked about sex for breakfast, sex for lunch, and sex for supper.

No, this was not some newfangled fantasy---we had been asked to bond as two proposed contributors for a crap local newspaper: Insight City News.

The editor thought (I am assuming) that we could blend well by virtue of being diametrically opposed in lifestyle and of course gender.

Two voices---one theme...a bit like Sonny and Cher.

He (the contributor) was in the throes of writing a book ('100 sexual positions') and was anxious to bring the meeting of fine minds to a close.

He had one week to write 15,000 words, but as a seasoned journalist that would be a piece of piss.

I ran past him various ideas and subject matters I had submitted to the editor: 'Bit of a bugger I can't use the 'HOW TO GET A FREEBIE FROM A SEX WORKER one' I said, 'that would have been a corker'.

I mentioned it because only a few days ago, this had actually been achieved.

Suddenly, 'Mr seasoned journalist' was not so hurried.

'Jesus' he boasted 'I can get free EVERYTHING......C.Ds', Books, Booze, clothes.....tell me how to do it...that's the only thing I DON'T know how to get!!!!'

'Would you like me to give you the bloke's number?' I joked, 'not only did he crack it....he cracked it with ME!!!!!'

Not so much: 'The unsinkable Molly Brown' but 'unreachable Alcatraz'

It took the bugger well over 7 months ...yes 7 MONTHS the clever sod.

He started with an approach on my website and the start of his crusade was shaky.

'Saw you on the street the other day....YOU WAS SHORTER THAN I IMAGINED'.

I was moved to respond that 'I may be short sunshine, but what I lack in height I make up for in personality'.

He also requested/gave me instructions as to the outfit he would love for me to replicate on my extensive photo gallery.

I won't relay the dog's dinner he had in mind, but you will get the gist when I say I replied with: 'Am actually attempting to attract the men TO me....rather than making them run for the hills'

I think you get the picture!!!!

He was RELENTLESS. If ever a bloke had mastered the art of tenacity and 'wearing the damsels down' he was the hardiest honcho by far.

We were all thrust and parry, like email fencing musketeers.

He attacked, I demurred, he delved deeper I then retreated.

On Guard, Epee, Touché.......

He tested the juices by sending a photo of himself. I didn't quite vomit, so he was clear to circle the amorous airport with a view to landing, if not between my thighs, my Egyptian cotton sheets.

He asked about me, my life and my ethos, and when he overstepped the mark (by sayin' somethin' stoopid).....he had a smooth line in self-deprecation, pathetic apology and was contrite, until it was safe to carry on in his quest.

He got drunk a few time and the carefully constructed veneer of just two people chatting was smeared with the inevitability of 'the real agenda'.

He showed acts of kindness, made sure I knew that women told him he was 'good in bed' and asked what qualities my ideal man would have.

'LOOK' I explained 'A MAN IS EITHER A LOVER OR A PATRON.....AND SINCE YOU ARE MARRIED (told me from the get go)....and since you have this 'thing about paying for it' (never quite found out what THAT was about though maybe the Irish Catholic thing was it) you have nowhere to go petal' was the kernel of my argument. This obviously fell on 'ears that want to hear the reverse'.

He laid siege to my ramparts with renewed vigour.

Then, he delivered the masterstroke. One keeps friends close and enemies/adversaries even closer, and he had found my weakest link: ROCK MUSIC.

I was lacking, and therefore, had a longing to hear, several A/C D/C C.D s', and he was willing, nay, he DEMANDED that he be allowed to fill my musical hole.

This was kismet and a pivotal point. I was reminded of the movie 'High Fidelity' where the offer of a musical compilation was a blatant statement of intent.

There would probably be no turning back.

It was of course a perfidious 'Trojan Horse'(I wonder if they named the condoms for that very reason), moving in by stealth and gaining a back door entrance into the city...until parked up all jolly in the meat market square.

Very cleverly, he chose not to meet me....he delivered them to my building while I was out instead.

AAAAAaaaahhh...how fucking sweet could you get????

He suggested meeting and I assented.

He continued to be helpful, an indispensable part of my daily life....like the postman's early morning delivery, or the unmistakeable and reassuring clink of the milkman's bottles.

Then an opening appeared for the bright young lad.

He offered technical help with my computer. Fluffy techno phobic bimbos are an easy mark and he took full advantage.

The visit coincided with a non-working day (for me) and we subsequently talked bollocks for 7 hours.

There was only a half-hearted semi grope on his departure

He naturally needed to continue said technical support a few days later and we talked bollocks for another 5 hours (there's only so much bollocks you can talk about) and he somehow resisted the urge to replicate previous lunge.

We somehow manufactured a reason for him visiting within the next few days.

Now by this time, I had wanked myself to death (my clitoris recoiling in horror every time my hand came near) and I suspect he had jerked his turgid member in many monumental tugs of war.

THIS was to be my knight in shining armour. He gave me the name of his accountant. I thought: 'if it's good enough for him, then I will give it a bash'

'He (the accountant) is totally straight, don't lie to him, he is not going to judge you, give him all the information you have and let the figures work for you' he kindly advised.

One doesn't need much of an imagination to know how the initial foray into the arcane world of 'going straight' went:

I dialled and stated: 'I would like to speak to Mr BS ('Bed Sheet') please'

Wouldn't you just know it, I got that bog standard, infuriating, bloomin': 'Learned at the school for dubious charm, Secretary Boot Camp' reply.

'WHAT'S IT REGARDING?' she asked

'Look' I longed to scream 'I'm in enough trouble with withering officialdom without YOU starting' Instead, I meekly explained I needed a bad motherfucker where accounting was concerned, and I had reason to believe that her boss was that very man.

She (I imagined) slowly filed her last nail....and mercifully stopped my already engorged aorta from imploding with frustration...and put me through.

'Hello' said an affable sounding young man who had no idea what he was about to take on.

Many people may think accountancy is a dull job, but for Mr BS, that was ALL about to change

My financial history was as complicated as the plot for: 'THE BIG SLEEP'.

(Even though Humphrey Bogart was one of my most favourite (nostalgic) actors, I couldn't make head OR tail of this movie plot.)

Hopefully Mr BS (nicknamed 'bed sheet' to rhyme with 'spread sheet' geddit?) would be adept at navigating the mind boggling maze, for he was going to have his work cut out.

First I had to convince him I was not a mad woman. Frankly, this was going to be tough.

'And when was your last return?'

'I've never made a return in this country'.

A predicable intake of breath and a leaden silence ensued.

'And your last period of taxable employment was with which employer?'

'Her Majesty's Inspector of Taxes'

Another pregnant pause stretched into the distance.

'And that was?'

'30 years ago'.

We did the deep breath, silence thing a few times. It became pellucid as to the QUAGMIRE of my taxable life.

The poor man!

I felt I was on trial before I had even started with the dreaded HMRC.

We eventually made an appointment, though guardedly (and I didn't blame him) he told me he needed 'a few days' to consider the size of the problem he was to face.

In retrospect, I would not have blamed him if he had left the office and disappeared like Reginald Perrin.

There was nothing straightforward about my Tax history, along with my life.

I had been outside the system for so long, what with my jolly jaunts world wide, it was a devil of a job convincing anyone who could help me, of my credulity.

I felt I should make a very important call to my plumber the next day. I asked him in all seriousness if he could plumb a toilet into the common hallway where the mailboxes were located.

'Why on earth would you need that?' he asked.

'BECAUSE EVERY MORNING WHEN I CHECK MY POST I LITERALLY SHIT MYSELF----I JUST WANT TO CUT OUT THE MIDDLE MAN'

NOT TONIGHT, I HAVE A HEADACHE

Interrogators and governmental sadists are well aware of the progress that can be made, when the culprit is the subject of sleep deprivation. Add to that, a chronic migraine, acute anxiety and a general lack of will to live and the prosecutors have an unfair advantage.

It was in this state that I was supposed to collate an entire lifetime's (all right---slight exaggeration) bungled bundle of financial information, so that I could give my brave accountant the best possible start with the 'battle of the bastards'

It took WEEKS. I found myself thinking 'what is the point in all of this, it doesn't MATTER: NOTHING, PIGGING WELL MATTERS.'

I accumulated the painstaking audit of my primary utilities and outgoings. In doing so, I realised why I never had any 'readies', even though on the days I bestowed noblesse oblige upon the horny, I felt I 'worked hard for the money.'

My cost of living was so high, I would have been better off going on the dole!!

Giving myself time off for bad behaviour, I walked down 'my manor'--- the road I negotiate nearly every day.

'Why do you swagger' someone once asked.

I was affronted by the observation. 'I stride purposefully' I chided.

'But you look so stuck up' they parried.

I had to explain that since time immemorial, with my lack of height, I had to assume the posture of someone taller.

That meant a certain 'shoulders back, tits out, glower at the universe' kind of countenance. It often was mistaken for arrogance or pride with a touch of snootiness thrown in.

This gait was now replaced by a fearful, uncertain wreck. It was not lost on Mike, a regular shopkeeper with whom I had a daily banter.

'What's wrong, you sumptuous hunk of woman hood?' he trilled.

I delayed the answer until I had my greasy sweaty mitts on the object of my affection.

'Bona Foodie', my local deli, had something I wanted and desired.

It was one of the only things that (still) brought a faint smile to my lips. The reason being: the olfactory glands are the keenest of the five senses, and this great emporium had something I both craved and that made me nostalgic for better days.

It was IMPORTED LIQUORICE and it transported me back to the glorious carefree days of Sydney, Australia, back in the Eighties.

My mates in Australia---and not an inconsiderable corresponding number in the UK, had dined out on 'The Liquorice story' for YEARS.

Why should *they* have all the fun?

There were eighty reasons why I had such a high standard of living, in Australia.

They were the number of hours I sometimes toiled (and I DO mean: back breaking, sweat inducing: *'hard yakka'*) for a number of months in Sydney.

On my days off, I would traditionally ensconce myself in the Palm Court of The Intercontinental Hotel, sip copious amounts of the finest champagne bubbles, and listen to the live classical quartet who performed there daily.

On this particular day I was wearing the finest apparel hard earned money could buy. There was a shop in Pitt St called: *'MERIVALE'*, they imported the very best/stylish clothes from all over the world.

I was swathed in designer white from head to toe, along with sheer fully fashioned white stockings and embroidered suspenders...... finished with zebra/ocelot stilettos.

The *Janet Reger* lace cami knickers were on this auspicious and very hot day, conspicuous by their absence.

It came time to leave, and the Concierge duly ordered me a taxi, but what eventually arrived was NOT a rust bucket radio cab.

A beautiful stretch limo, also in white, awaited madam.

It was their (the bell boys') gift to me. Every week I always called into 'Centerpoint Tower' to pick up some of their favourite confectionary: 'Darryl Lee Liquorice'---and I ALWAYS declined to take their money.

So for this Act of kindness, I was today, travelling home in style.

The scrummy driver (we all love a man in uniform) seemed like a nice boy, and since I wasn't in a hurry to go straight home to a domestic argument with my current beau (I was already late)--I decided I may as well be hung for a bloody great sheep as a lamb

'Let's go to the Botanical Gardens and watch the sun go down (no pun), maybe we can crack open another bottle and watch a 'bluey' (porn movie) in the back seat' I enthused.

He naturally thought it was a brilliant idea. There is nothing better than getting laid and paid (as I keep bragging to people), so he loved the double whammy of knowing that I was a 'pro' (the staff told him), therefore he would have the distinction of 'getting it for free'.

Little things please little minds.

Several glasses/(bottles) imbibed over the course of the afternoon meant that I desperately required a 'toilet break', and even though the gardens were 'chocca' with the horseshoe shape of parked limos, I figured I could retain a MODICUM of modesty by squatting beside the car with my bottom pointing out to the Sydney Opera House.

As stated previously, being able to release 10 gallons of stored up urine has GOT to be up there in the: 'This is so fan-fucking-tastic' stakes of sheer relief.

I started 'PUSHING' the flow out in ecstasy, and on looking down (to make sure I was not splashing my feet) I was nonplussed to see, in the barely lit dusk, the spreading black fluid of an unfortunate accident.

I HAD FOLLOWED THROUGH.

'If farts have lumps' the saying goes 'you have certainly shit yourself'.

But it was not just over my feet. By virtue of the tightness of my skirt, I had soiled my pristine clothes, the lower half of my body, and so large was my accident, practically from front to back wheel of the Limo!!!!!!

I may as well have fallen into a three feet high cow pat.

You may well laugh folks, I had a handsome *good sort* 'hot to trot', (he had already relocated from front to back of the limo) who was well on the way to stroking his 'tool of oppression' in readiness for an evening of impromptu passion.

I banged on the back door of the car----hoping that he would not smell the rising smell of noxious fumes.

'You got any tissues?' I croaked nervously

He jumped back into the front and opened the glove compartment.

What he gave me was: A snow white, monogrammed and delicately embroidered/lacy (must have come from Bruges), lovingly laundered and pressed Hankie.

Talk about giving strawberries to pigs.

I game fully tried to stem the tide of Darryl Lee effluent, (for sure, THAT was the culprit), but I may as well have tried to mop up the Sydney Harbour with a cotton bud.

Thinking on my feet, or in this case squatting and covered with half a litre of shit, I called on a common female untruth.

'Would you mind if we went straight home' I pleaded, 'I've just started my period'

This disgruntled driver dressed himself, returned to his driver's seat (which was thankfully approx 100yards from my passenger seat) and I slid/squelched into the back of my mobile 'portaloo'.

He switched on the ignition, paused..........and said........

COULD I HAVE MY HANKIE BACK?

Aaahhh, those were the days!!!!

But 'the days of wine and roses are not long' as they say.

Back to the car crash of my nefarious life, I considered wearing panty pads as a precaution against my bowels permanently turning to water.

LIFE IN THE PAST LANE

'Who d'ya reckon dobbed you in to the HMRC???' was the first question raised by most misguided, well-meaning Samaritans. They figured (and I concurred) that HMRC were so useless they could not have arrived at my door without help.

Frankly my dear, I didn't give a damn. It would be disingenuous to waste vital energy even PONDERING the vexing question.

Julie Burchill (I'm reliably informed), used to opine: 'There are civilians and then there's us.' Where normal thought processes were concerned.

I found it thought provoking that anyone would waste an idiotic second on needing to know who the Judas was in their midst.

It really did not MATTER. Energy was needed for fighting the authorities and not some imaginary 'dob a hooker' arse wipe.

However, if I found the slime ball they would indubitably be hexed for life.

We ARE a terrible nation of snitchers, the people in the South East being the very worst!

Unfortunately, HMRC actively RELY on disgruntled partners, punters, or just nasty people with a grudge.

I read with interest that: '40,000 people have anonymously rung the Government's Tax Evasion hotline, since it was launched last April.' A spokesman for HMRC said it was impossible to take action against

people who rang with false info.

He said: 'If we asked people to leave their name and address, many would be reluctant to give us the information'

No shit Sherlock. Oh well, that's ok then!!!!!!

The Government must be very proud to use the publics' basest instinct, as in: REVENGE, to reap money.

Police state Britain really sucked.

'Ooooooooh, Gawd' I groaned one day to nobody in particular, 'Please, pretty please, God…..tell me I have not tickled a Tax inspector or rimmed a Revenue man' .

They undoubtedly COULD have rung for 'details'.

What if they had invested £200 (or more) in sending a Tax spy to quiz me during my Body Worship service??

The thought appalled me until I boned up on THE LAW.

That, (I felt) would have technically been 'entrapment' but I STILL was paranoid about unexplained clicks on the phone and strangers taking my photo (as usual) from across Marine Parade, with a long lens, mega professional looking camera.

Any customer with an unhealthy interest in: The time I had lived in Brighton, whether I had a second residence, the cost of ANYTHING in my abode or my outgoings (bloody cheek) ----I froze and became defensive and utterly frosty.

They were not the questions that a person hoping for a good seeing to would normally ask.

Bed Sheet, my accountant (he finally assented to taking me on) emailed with a list of requirements for another million pieces of personal information.

I tore my flat apart looking for any scraps of paper that might be useful, and thanked God that I was a complete slut where house work was concerned.

I found a few years' appointment/diary books, my Roget's Thesaurus, and photos I hadn't seen for years. They were images of a happier carefree time.

I found a dodgy 'Animal Farm' movie and a few ancient Birthday cards. It seems I was born the year they invented the teabag.

I also found I had a general Malaise which made the arduous task almost impossible.

In the meantime I had sifted through all of my friends' pieces of information and advice.

'For Christ sake don't go into your interview with hot shot KPMG tax accountants, they will skin you alive' cautioned my dear mate Kei.

'Why?' I asked

'I have a friend who used to be an Inspector and that is one thing they hate above all. If you show you have £600 an hour to fritter away they will crush you like a Cockroach----I'm urging you DON'T DO IT!'

That made sense, but another gem of wisdom (from someone who had been investigated and had eventually (just) lived to tell the tale) did not make sense: 'WHATEVER you do, make sure you don't get a woman investigator----even INSIST upon it being a man!!

'Women are evil bitches, and because of the nature of your work they will be unfairly prejudiced' he told me in benevolent tones.

'And the Lesbians are even worse' he added as an afterthought

I didn't entirely agree. The sales of my books were heart-warmingly embraced by the female sex and Gay Men/women. The problem was: I had asked so many people for so many points of view, that I didn't know my own mind any more. I had to get back to basics.

I idly flicked through my book and with horror saw there was more than one mention of the dreaded Taxman.

OOOOh, NO!!!!!

I certainly didn't appear to be very complimentary, though this was more to do with my state of mindless boredom when in their employ than anything else.

This was going to be a delicious kismet for them.

I remembered going for my interview at the then titled: Her Majesty's Inspector of Taxes governmental building in Cambridge.

A bleak H block of ancient defunct army barracks (now condemned and demolished) was the address.

I wore a set of 'Fred Astaire' Coat Tails, a black and white striped shirt complete with velvet tie.

My 'loon pants' were a scary 3 feet wide. I topped the ensemble with 6" high platform shoes.

Two sets of false eyelashes adorned my upper eyelid, with individual false lashes on the bottom lid.

I was the only colourful thing in the place.

AND I STILL GOT THE JOB!!!!!

You cannot tell me that they were not aware of what they were getting.

It was a miserable soul sapping gig for which I was utterly unsuited. Three years of relentless tedium and toil as a Clerical Assistant, reduced me to a catatonic state of mind. I hated my job but I was so unhappy I did not know how to break the cycle of boredom.

I rebelled by using the 'flexi-time' to such a degree that I was only suffering three and a half hours a day. I was regularly sent home for 'being inappropriately dressed' ….the T shirt bearing the legend: 'NIGEL IS A WANKER' was badly received.

Well it wasn't like they didn't have an inkling of my penchant for individuality clothes wise.

My body bothered them. My breasts were then, like the continental shelf (big and perky) and my clothes merely accentuated the fact.

My boobs are always getting me in trouble. I latterly (in 2007) wrote one of my numerous 'Web-logs' about it entitled: 'Get yer tits out for the lads'.

It follows:

'A few years ago, I felt that body fascism had reached its nadir---I looked down from my eerie, overlooking the pavement, and saw: A WANKING MAN.

The ultimate irony was not lost on me. Don't laugh, but I felt a mixture of annoyance, impotence, revulsion and I also felt a tad frightened (titter ye not)

The guy had obviously seen me sitting on the balcony, though in no way was I in such a state of nudity to warrant such attention.

I was quite happily reading about how the Hang Seng and Dow Jones had added 300 points overnight and that the 'Footsie' was at an all-time high (pushing the 7000 barrier)---when my attention was drawn to a car that was parked on the road, but blocking the entrance to the next door's forecourt.

'He'd better move before the 'curtain twitchers' run out to him' I thought.

He appeared to be having trouble winding up what appeared to be a very stiff window.

On closer inspection, I could see that it wasn't the window which was enjoying the wrist action--- and as for what WAS being tugged, turgidity was not in question.

I rang the police.

'There's a guy masturbating outside my flat' I complained

'Is he engaged in this activity on your property madam?' the call -centre 'by the book' guy replied.

'He's in his car, on the near side of the road---looking up at me---and he's erm, you know touching his man -bits'

'So he's not in fact trespassing then Madam' said their call centre dolt who was in danger of me crawling down the phone wire and ripping out his throat

'Well no, but surely he is contravening certain anti-social behaviour as in 'lewd in public' or something' I snapped

He droned on about this that and the other, but was not telling me what I wanted to hear. I mean, even the bird from Eastenders got done for fellating her OWN boyfriend in public.

'In which case, I will just have to go down there myself' I stated petulantly.

'I strongly advise you not to do that Madam, he may be armed'

Ha!! Well his weapon was neither dangerous nor concealed---and that was my very point.

'Perhaps if you go inside for a while, he will leave of his own accord' Mr impassive and impervious suggested.

Drawing breath to remonstrate, I realised that this is what the crime is all about---it's about power.

So I bade farewell to 'Mr useless as tits on a tomato' and cowered, yes COWERED behind my drapes until the bastard had either left or finished the 'job in hand'

After a while the coast was clear and I took up my position on my balcony once more.

5 minutes later the repeat offender was back, either to polish off the previous job or to restart another.

I withdrew back inside and rang the police once again.

I got the same phone controller.

We pretty much went laboriously through the former conversation until he said:

'You must be doing something to incite the guy'

When I had finally picked myself up from the floor of incredulity and taken any hint of umbrage from the timbre of my voice, I told him calmly and concisely what I was wearing: SARONG FROM WAIST TO FLOOR--AND MATCHING *TRES* ATTRACTIVE BIKINI TOP.

One would think that this was perfectly acceptable sunbathing apparel on a torrid day where the mercury was hitting 90'. 'Are you --what I mean to ask is----bosom wise-----do you-----HAVE YOU GOT A LARGE BUST madam?'

I told him I did, and also informed him that as far as I knew---THERE WAS NO LAW AGAINST HAVING BIG TITS.

He GRUDGINGLY ACCEPTED THIS STATEMENT.

But the subtext/unspoken twaddle was: 'If you have massive mammary glands, what do you expect'

So that's O.K. then.

Beaten into submission by horny man's inability to stop playing with him self when confronted with bewitching jugs?

WELL PAINT ME BLACK AND CALL ME BWANA!!

I'm going to get one of those protective splatter guards (like Lady Di had when going into the bomb disposal zone) and I will fry my baps on my balcony with impunity.

If the plonkers make a habit of it, I WILL post their number plate to the cops, just so they can get an official warning.

Even better, I fantasised about getting friendly official help with regard to addresses matching *DVLA* records.

I just want to see the look on the twit's face when I rock up and start 'touching myself inappropriately' whilst opposite HIS house.

I will of course make sure that I am not on his property.

THAT WOULD BE AGAINST THE LAW.

One thing is for sure, my breasts may have been the cause of many an altercation in the past, but lamentably they were NOT going to get me out of this mess!!!!

BEANIE FLICKERS AND BEAN COUNTERS

My appointment was fixed to see my 'Innumeracy saviour'.

I was recognisant of the fact that I HAD to tell him the truth about EVERYTHING.

It would not be fair to a person who was held in high regard, to be dragged down by the act of being a figures' man for an 'intimacy facilitator'…and for her figures to be fallacious. I was NOT going to let my guy down!

I stuffed my entire financial history into a portmanteau and off I set. I rang Miss 'how to win friends and influence people' and asked where the offices were located.

She disinterestedly gave me the name of the road.

'And the Number is?' I enquired.

'It doesn't have a number'

'Well how am I supposed to locate you?'

'It's a big white building'.

Boy, this insouciant 'front person' of a large accountancy firm was twanging my last jangled nerve.

I had no fight left in me and conceded defeat. I hoped the Cabbie had done 'The Knowledge'

More by accident than design, I arrived to a complicated: 'press button and the door will open, then pull TOWARDS you' scenario.

I introduced myself to my nail filing tormenter and made a stumbling bumbling hash of it.

'Letitcia for Mr BS' I announced cheerily.

I thought: 'If she chuffing well asks 'what's it regarding' one more time, I will not be responsible for the damage I will do in a cat fight'.

'I can't see your name' she responded suspiciously.

'Oh, it must be my REAL name I'm under…….the other was my STAGE name'.

She looked even MORE suspicious.

'Bed Sheet' rescued me from being quizzed, as he arrived in reception to greet me.

There seemed to be a suspicious number of employees milling around the water cooler and others coincidentally happening to be in the corridor looking industrious with sheaves of paper.

'Perhaps they have never seen a real live prostitute before' I mused to myself.

It was like a bearded lady from the circus coming to visit them, sparing them a trip to the Big Top.

'Bed Sheet' set such a cracking pace walking ahead of me up the stairs, that he failed to notice that my financial history was weighing me down in the PHYSICAL sense.

It was not as such, an un-chivalrous act. It was probably six of my heightened state of hysteria, and half a dozen of him trying to run for the hills while there was still time.

He had drafted in some hot shot tax accountants from London to sit in on the meeting since he 'had not dealt with an investigation at this level'.

What stratospheric level was that?

Crumbs!!! Was it REALLY that bad?

We started a tenuous bonding over a cup of tea, and I surveyed the picture of his family----prominently placed on the desk, as if (in my imagination) to ward off the 'evil whore she devil spirit' in his midst!

Then the heavyweight Yodas of the Tax world arrived with bulging briefcases and a fearsome handshake which meant: 'We are mean bastards and we play to win'

One WAS from KMPG, but I remembered Kei's advice 'They (HMRC) will crush you like a cockroach'.

They were good cop/bad cop. One all flinty eyed and steel rimmed glasses and the other was benevolent and exuded kindness.

This really was not the time or place to say to 'Flinty': 'Er, hang on---haven't we met before?' but I never forget a face I sat on and my thighs (I thought) had DEFINITELY grazed his eyes!!!!!

Talk about Six degrees of separation of Salvador Dali proportions!!!!!!!

They immediately proved their 'All see, all knowing' status by pointing out a name and case number which was located in the bottom left hand corner of my original 'less than love-letter'. In my hysteria, I had completely overlooked it.

GRABINER/case no/Letitcia

'You're a 'Grabiner' case' they informed me.

Even 'bed sheet', did not know the significance of the name.

Yes, a character called Lord Grabiner QC was drafted in by Gordon Brown to bring the 'informal economy' into the loving open arms of the Authorities. I was not sure if this was portentous.

I searched the net for anything which would give me an insight into the Modus Operandi of Grabby Baby.

It seems the primary concern of Grabiner cases, was to steam in hard and prosecute (where before this had not been the case), extract extortionate amounts of money through heavy penalties and introduce bailiffs to take your possessions if one had nothing to give financially.

In short they were heartless merciless heavies who had the power to metaphorically suck you dry.

'They always win their cases and they are prepared to spend 97p to get

3p in the pound' said Mr (very familiar) Man of steel.

The meeting seemed like a precursor to a sodding Criminal Court Case.

For the tenth time in as many days, I recounted my peripatetic movements around the globe, question after question, designed (I suppose) to trip me up and expose a hint of LIAR.

Courts could assume that I was a lying Prossie who was not to be trusted, since that is the general perception of the uneducated and the ignorant, so maybe they had to test how I would stand up to quick fire scrutiny.

I guess they were only trying to ascertain my veracity and validating my trustworthiness. I felt my cheeks burn with indignation. They were supposed to be the good guys!!! My life had more twists and turns than a F.1 race track. Nothing was straightforward. No week month or year bore any relation, rhyme or reason to that which had gone before or after.

'What are your total assets' asked Mr 'kind and gentle'

I wanted to say: 'My eternal optimism, my tits ......and the ability to deep throat and lick gonads at the same time'

Instead I listed the current roll call of revenue.

There was an air of expectancy in the grilling room.

Ah!!!!---so THIS was what it was all about.

By trying to explain to 'Bed Sheet' in earlier phone conversations the fact that I was not some 'skag head' from the street, or a two liner in a massage section, I had name dropped assiduously: 'Cynthia Payne' (because I vaguely knew her) and Lindi St Clair (because I vaguely knew about her court case).

They thought I was minted!!!!!

Keith's pen was poised to deliver them the mother lode, they were already buying a second villa in the Tuscan hills.

'Sixty odd quid in Bank account one, fifty in Bank account two, and the bulk (not even enough for a deposit on a beach hut) in number three' was my opening disclosure.

They leaned closer, with untold riches a mere second away.

'I have a couple of grand's worth of equity shares' I continued

They leaned closer still.

'And finally, about 4,500 unsold Body Worship books that are sitting like a bowl of milk in a warehouse somewhere-----AND THAT'S IT!!!!!!'

Keith' pen was STILL all poise and purpose and they were by now practically sitting on my lap, they were willing me to tell them more, they obviously EXPECTED me to reveal the treasure of the Sierra Madre.

Alas this was not the case.

They had endured a wasted rail journey on a wild loose woman chase.

'Bed sheet' looked embarrassed and they, in turn, looked deflated and then all started looking at one another in incredulity.

'YOU ARE GOING TO NEED LEGAL AID' said 'Mr disappointed to have to take the Ferrari back to the showroom'.

'Okay' I brightened, 'how do I get that?'

'You cannot actually GET legal aid for a case of this magnitude' he explained.

Everyone was looking mighty worried, and when they started speaking in tongues: I.e.: Legal jargon like 'Maximum 7 years' incarceration', 'Move to Hansard and away from criminality' I started to well up like a big girlie's blouse.

They started coughing uncomfortably and shuffling their papers BACK into their less than reassuring cases. They were leaving.

'BUT YOU HAVE TO HELP ME' I wailed.

They said they would 'ask around' and 'see what they could do' and GAVE ME THEIR CARD---in case I knew anyone (preferably mega stupid and rich) who was in of need their expertise. And then they were gone, leaving a quaking Letitcia and a disquiet laden 'bed sheet'.

He finally asked: 'Who did you say recommended you again?' and I fleetingly thought back to the 'freebie monster' who vouchsafed for him.

HE SHOOTS AND HE SCORES

After a tortuous courtship the 'freebie eejit' arrived for his 'prize' and the pragmatic, sensible part of my brain still said NO, yet my especially shaved 'front botty' screamed 'take me and do your worst you filthy Drongo'.........

I was up to my tits in 'other stuff to do' on this day of all days. I had to do an unpaid quick BBC Southern Counties radio sound bite (in my elevated position as omnipotent oracle) regarding the big news of the day: The arrival/proposal of new sex laws, as in 'mini brothels'.

However, that was HOURS away. It transpired that I needed every minute.

And so, the moment of: Can we (jointly) possibly live up to the expectation of the fantasy that had undoubtedly formed in both our ardent minds.

That would surely be impossible, and so it proved.

The fault could be equally divided. It was so WRONG, WRONG, MOTHER FUCKING WRONG!!!!!

Wrong of HIM to eat Garlic the day before the Big Match (he was a footie fan)

Wrong of ME, to take my kit off (home strip), in an exasperated (at being finally caught): 'lets just get this 'shomozzle' out of the way shall we' fashion.

Wrong of HIM, to touch me the way he had touched his missus for the last 15-20 years. It seemed we were not physiologically built the same, and anyway, the 4-3-4 formation went out with the ark.

Wrong of HIM to bollock- ache about: 'bloody condoms'. A ruck with the opposing team is a yellow card offence. He continually attempting to push the rigid boundaries of my rigorous 'mega safe sex policy'(and NO, he did not succeed)

Wrong of ME: not to have had a 'gutbuster breakfast' (Shades of Glenn Hoddle's nutritionist) to give me the energy which seemed required by this selfish twat.

Wrong of HIM not to take direction (TRAINING SESSIONS ARE SO IMPORTANT) when I pointed out the obvious as in: 'Do this sunshine, and do not in any way prevaricate or meander away from the tried and means tested orgasmic path.'

This he did continually in a: 'I know what I'm doing sweet pea' kinda way.

Wrong of ME not to just switch the floodlights off and abandon the fixture with teargas on the terraces and shit loads of riot police TRYING

VALIANTLY TO RESTORE ORDER and control the capacity crowd.

Wrong of HIM to have that faintly smug 'GOTCHA' look (like Beckham), with the insolent 'I've got my feet firmly under your table' countenance.

Wrong of ME not to just give him a slap...or at least the 'hair dryer treatment' A La Fergie the Manchester United boss.

Wrong of HIM not to BEHAVE (think Gazza), and not to follow the requisite 1hr preparation time written in 'bedroom etiquette' where a potential fisting is concerned.

It was wrong of ME, to be doing it at all.

In my 'cup (but not WORLD cup) half full, rather than half empty world', I tried to focus on anything that I could find that was in any way GOOD about it.

I had to search really hard.

Why, oh why, had we embarked on this misguided ascent of *Everest*?

What had seduced us into this fumbling folly?

Me, a Tensing Norgay to his Sir Edmund Hillar(y)ious...the blind leading the blind up the most dangerous circuitous route....without appropriate training, crampons and safety ropes????

On that torpid mountain we were running out of time and good light, the weather was closing in and the high altitude was making it difficult to breath.

It looked for the world as if it was going to be a goalless draw, with extra time the 'golden boot' and a pigging penalty shoot out.

I hadn't sprinted up and down the pitch all day long....... JUST TO END UP HAVING A WANK.

Out of my mind and out of ideas in this war of attrition I tried one more time to convey in clear helpful instructions how he could enable my pent up river to burst the banks.

'HOW ABOUT YOU JUST LICK ME LIKE A DOG...BUT LEAVE THE BARKING BIT OUT?' I guided.

Any NORMAL man would think 'Shit I'd better do as I'm told'.

Not this Eejit, for only the BIGGEST EEJIT OF ALL would enquire as to the length of time this particular procedure would take.

Now there is a time for black humour and a time to err very clearly on the side of conservatism. Biggus- Dickus -Headus's timing was way off.

How in the name of a Rhino's rectum I achieved 'girlie ghee' is between me and the outrageous (sick) thoughts that ran through my depraved mind.

I had finally landed on the orgasmic tarmac with all the exhaustion of a London-Sydney flight. I had 'pet lag' and had barely cleared customs when I had to jump on another flight.

IT WAS A 747-400 JUMBO

It's said that size doesn't matter, though the Ad men assert that it

DOES.

I personally don't give a toss..........BUT........

If skating judges were to score the 'appendage de jour' it would have been shades of Torvill and Dean....PERFECT 6's all round.

Credit where credit is due...there has to be a silver lining round the cumulous cloud.

He had the most perfectly formed dick I had ever seen.

SNIFFING OUT A LEGAL BEAGLE

'We have found a man to tick all the boxes' 'Bed Sheet' trilled, in a call a few days after the meeting from hell.

'Well a man who can tick my box is welcome news indeed' I thought

This was more like it!!! He was a partner in a well known Law firm (I checked his impeccable credentials), and through some happenstance and legal convolution, he somehow was prepared to ride shotgun for my shaky stagecoach---for FREE.

I assented to him being my insulation and membrane against the elements, and to ringing Ms Frick (the investigator) and finding out what was what.

My hero!!!! He would protect me and make everything all right. He would place Germaline and bandages over the festering gaping hole that served as my life.

He rang me. I COULD NOT UNDERSTAND A WORD HE SAID.

It wasn't that he spoke Swahili or Mandarin. His impeccable credentials also crept into his speech patterns and oral delivery (Oh missus). They were clipped, bristling with authority and barely audible.

My hearing is shaky due to Monsters of Rock concerts making my ears bleed at concerts, or via the full blast settings on my earphones.

We were not a match made in litigation heaven.

His voice reminded me of horny would be customers, making covert whispered calls while ensconced in the men's room of their Employer.

We fixed an appointment to meet at his office in London.

As usual I eschewed the notion of 'Monica Lewinsky dress code while going to court' apparel. It was leopard print hat and papal (irreverent) purple for me. I had lost my mind or sense of any future.

No sense in losing my inimitable sense of panache fashion wise as well!!!!!

First, I swung by The Covent Garden Hotel, in Monmouth St, just to see 'my boys', the Concierge.

Especially, I hoped, the attractive young 'Timbo'.

I stayed at the hotel when I had the 'London Launch' for my book Body Worship (2005), and these guys were a witness to my disgraceful over imbibing. They helped to scrape both me, and a hangover from the bowels of hell, into a Taxi when I returned to Brighton.

I remembered saying to one of them when I arrived as a hotel guest one year before: 'There you go possum (I gave him a crisp £20)—your arse is mine'.

Being the epitome of the great Aussie larrikin, they understood that I was asking them to look after me. I need not have bothered with money.

They were a breed of Employee which every service cries out for; efficient, engaging and eager to please. They would have made terrific sex workers.

They were all there and remembered me, my ebullience and my book. I gave them a copy as part of my gratuity!!!!

'Waddya up to?' they enquired in their sing song Aussie 'Strine'.

'Oh look, don't even ask---I'm in the middle of the most AWFUL Tax investigation and criminal prosecution'

They were sweet and attentive as always, and guided me to a table in their restaurant.

An exquisitely dressed man was sitting at the bar and was unabashedly STARING in my direction. When it was time for my appointment with the 'Whore Whisperer' he approached my table.

'Are you English?' he asked.

'English Irish actually' I replied.

'It's just that you look absolutely wonderful, not many British women dress up these days you know'.

I started to feel a waterfall of tears spring to the surface of my eyes, and forcing them back I replied: 'you simply don't know how much I needed that compliment today of all days'.

'Why is that?'

'When I say Inland Revenue, you will get the picture' I sniffed knowingly.

He snorted with derision: 'NONSENSE my girl, it's only MONEY my dear, it's only MONEY. Just stay looking good, they can't take THAT away from you'. He then walked away, turned at the door and blew me a kiss.

I found the imposing building where my Legal Demi -God was housed and checked in at reception for security clearance. As I made my way to the elevators the security guard started (for no reason) humming the reggae tune: 'Don't worry, be happy'.

I got in the lift and as the door was about to close, I called out: 'Yes and the singer of that song allegedly bloody committed suicide!!!!!'

WW (Whore Whisperer) was all I expected and more. Attractive, polite, suited and booted. He exuded, nay, OOZED power, and was the kind of guy you needed fighting in your corner.

What with my accountant (Bed Sheet), I seemed to have stumbled on 'Team Letitcia'. They were my 'Two (w)hor(s)emen of the apocalypse' and I felt more than fortunate to have them.

He produced a 'Disclosure pack'. That was supposedly what the HMRC had as a nucleus or a foundation for their investigations.

There were no great surprises. My website, (along with my prices), my three bank accounts (like it's illegal to have three), and a huge five page interview I did with my local rag: The Argus, with the ridiculous headline: 'PUTTING THE SEX INTO SUSSEX.'

It is not a coincidence that it is sometimes knick named: 'The Anus'.

The reason being, the standard of journalism was very poor, in a 'never let the truth get in the way of a good story' kind of way.

I weighed up their evidence and felt strangely confident that it was all pants.

WW's practised eye swooped over my accounts. He was dismissive of their suspicions that I was some whopping great money launderer. He could see that there were no vast amounts going in or out of any of the accounts, and queried the need to either have a formal 'interview' under caution, or indeed to have an investigation, at that level, at ALL.

'Let's get that interview date changed' he soothed. We eventually arrived at June 22nd as the date of my demise at the clutches of the enemy.

As far as I could see there was nothing that screamed 'They have you by the lips of your labia'. I remembered the finished article of the Argus interview, it was published from 6th Aug to the 8th 2005 and THAT was the weekend of Gay Pride in Brighton.

One year earlier I had a 'gay weekend' of my own.

PORN TO BE MILD

I want to be Porn star' he exclaimed

I, on the other hand, wanted to have a few days away from the madness of Brighton Gay Pride--------

Previously, dear Al was the only Male Escort I knew who travelled 300 miles to see me with a dozen red roses and a cheeky little *rose champagne* in ice cooler----- complete with Lalique crystal glasses.

What a star!!! And I was the recipient.

I decided to go visit his home town in the hope that we could maybe link up again---and besides there were other attractions to the city of Birmingham.

There was another guy advertising his sexual services on the sex site: 'Adult Work', and his incessant texting, whilst irritating, had piqued my libidinal interest.

I let Virgin Trains take the strain, and ascertained from the buffet car operator that: 'there are more lap dancing clubs in Birmingham per square mile than anywhere in the U.K.'

I SAY!!!!

Perversity being my middle name (I had a dinner date with Al at 8.30) I nevertheless proceeded to ring proposed conquest number two, hoping I could 'squeeze him in' before fine dining.

He wanted to come straight to my hotel, but I wanted to get the lay of the terrain----and found myself wandering to a development called: The Mail Box.

Next door was Malmaison the bar- restaurant, and hotel.

What the hell, I was on 'ho holiday' and wandered in like John Wayne just rode into town. As is my wont, I ordered a glass of chilled rose champagne.

My waiter exclaimed: 'You're from Brighton aren't you?'

'Bloody hell', I thought 'I would make a dreadful career criminal---instantly recognisable from 4 hours worth of travel time'.

I watched the Friday lunchtime carousers gearing up for the big week end---and ordered another glass.

'Mr Adultwork' kept up the pressure text wise, but it was a beautiful day, I was free from the shackles of erotic service providing and the world was my lobster.

I eventually wandered (staggered) into the shopping complex and decided to have a late lunch, after all, I would need my energy!!!!

By the time I got back to Base I was knackered, and decided to have a

'Churchillian' power nap.

The 'text fiend' would just have to wait.

I roused from my slumber to find that I had 45 minutes to make a glamour transformation for the evening ahead. My phone registered frantic messages from Mr Text---and a moment of madness won.

'Never put off until tomorrow what you can do today' they say. Accordingly I put myself under the most heinous pressure, and said yes to my (for the past YEAR) ardent admirer. A quick text to tell Al I was running late.......but obviously omitting the reason why.

Mr ' Reason Why' rang the door- bell.

Nice.

Yes, very nice indeed.

I blurted, 'I don't have much time I'm going out soon'.

He was unfazed and proceeded to do to me what he had been threatening (boasting) he could do for the past year.

I'm pretty speedy out of the starting gate where achieving a climax is concerned, but if I'm under pressure I lose the plot. My gunpowder refuses to go of with a bang.

I squinted at the time showing on the Hotel TV.

BOLLOCKS!!!!! I was way behind schedule!!!

I employed every technique I knew in the time honoured fashion of tipping over the climax cliff, and was failing miserably. It wasn't the delivery of the pleasure (the boy did good), it was the knowing I had another cutie pie arriving at my hotel in 4 minutes.

I fantasised about cats (really) dogs (uh huh) big, small, old, young fat, thin, grotesques, borderline family members, scenes of unimaginable (apart from mine) depravity.

My legs and face were twitching and I felt as if the beat of my heart was at the zenith of heartbeats allowed before pulmonary embolism kicks in.

Bingo!!! What a relief, I allowed myself 20 seconds recovery and a 5 second cuddle. Big mistake, He wanted his *Quid pro quo* and I didn't have the time to reciprocate. His mood changed like a tropical rainstorm, and he left (as in, flounced out the door) on not the best of terms.

Al was waiting with a glass of chilled champagne downstairs and boy did I need it.

Dinner was a gastronomic delight at Brindley Place at a 2 Star Michelin (Raymond Blanc) joint.

Our second night of pleasure went even better than on Al's (paid) inaugural trip to Brighton and I showed him how to make it in the Porn world.

'Al, you are going to have to deliver the money shot when the director says: 'Go-Go-Go'....so let's practice' I said

I counted down from 20...and by 7 his ardour was in spurt mode.

'Whoa there, a bit premature petal' I cried.

'I thought you would be counting from 10' was his reply.

What a star. Cumming all over a TV screen soon no doubt!!!!

I was supposed to see him the next day, but he made a blunder of Nagasaki proportions: HE TOLD HIS PARENTS HE WANTED TO BE THE JOHN HOLMES OF THE WESTERN WORLD!!!!

They threw him out and I have never heard from him again.

SUMMERTIME AND THE LIVIN' IS QUEASY

I have been in a courtroom four times in my life.

The first time was as a rape attempt victim. The serial offender was found rightfully guilty, due in no small part, to the fact that he had 75 other crimes to be taken into consideration

The second was as a perceived miscreant who was swathed in the Queen's Jubilee (25th anniversary) bunting, and therefore deemed to have nicked it. I rightfully gained a conditional discharge.

The third was to act as character witness for a mate who had attempted holding up a newsagent with a toy pistol. My previous conditional discharge, though 6 years later, was still hanging over me and my friend went down for 4 years (it being a long time for ANYBODY to go down).

The fourth was to give evidence with regard to a Malay lady nicking my washing from the line at the Batu Ferringhi guest house where I lived. She made the mistake of WEARING it in George Town (17 Kilometres away), and since my clothes (non)sense proceeds me, they were instantly recognised by my guest house neighbours. She was found guilty.

They were my only terms of reference.

D day arrived on the 22nd June.

There was plenty of time for panic, and rising hysteria to take its deadly toll.

I was a mess.

Forget the proverbial lamb to the abattoir, I was a baby seal surrounded by a baker's dozen of heartless club wielding harridans.

Yep. I got WOMEN investigators. Yes indeed, there were TWO OF them!!!!!

I nicknamed them 'Frick and Frack' (after Kennedy's secret service police protectors) .

Mindful of my mate Kei's suggestion that I 'do humble' dress wise, I tried to convey a: 'just popping out to pick up the newspapers' look.

Humble I could do. Humiliation is another thing entirely.

To reach our interrogators, we had to walk through the open plan, ugly, and lifeless office which housed the Brighton branch of the dreaded fiscal fascists.

As in the initial interview with my accountant: loads of people were loitering with intent at the water cooler, and many were aimlessly strolling with a piece of paper.

'Not seen a real live one before?' I thought.

They had obviously never seen a hooker up close and personal, and they relished every second of my agony.

The Anti Fraud/criminal investigation squad did not come -a -callin' every week I'm sure. There would have been an unbearable 'frisson' in the otherwise drab and dreary life of a Tax Worker. Then, in walks the most instantly recognisable person in Brighton. ME.

I remembered Del Boy from 'Only fools and horses' advising his side kick to 'play it cool---play it cool' before falling in a heap the other side of the pub bar.

However, we made perfect entrance.

A pretty lady with opalescent eyes shook my brief's hand and mine. She was the name made flesh from my original 'billet deux'.

THIS was Ms 'Frick'

She was diminutive in stature and I prayed that she did not have a Napoleonic Syndrome-complex which slays all perceived felons.

Ms 'Frack' was a thin lipped 'bow-wow'.

It was beyond tantalising to whisper to WW: 'Jeez, I don't fancy YOURS much!'....but I mercifully refrained.

Into the 'interview room' we strode. For all intents and purposes, THIS was the 'police station'.

It was the financial equivalent of: 'helping the police with their enquiries', except in my case I would not be released without charge after a few hours. I was going to be made to suffer for careless remarks in my book, for non disclosure of revenue, and the non submission of earnings since Jason Donovan looked handsome and boyish.

It was a blur, filled with a legal ceremony of signing disclosures/statements and the breaking of cellophane on audio tapes. It was okay for my ultra cool Lawyer to sit there with a beatific smile on his face but this was my FIRST time at the rodeo.

I had suspicions that the 'Tax psychologist' had decreed that: 'All interviewees must suffer in heat no less than 45-50 degree Celsius.

'Blimey it's hot' I complained (legitimately)

The windows were smashed, even though we were one, or maybe even two floors up. Let's face it one would be hard pressed to find a more legitimate target!!!!

I didn't really know WHAT my rights were, but playing Alec Guinness in a modern re enactment of Bridge over the river Kwai (where he is incarcerated in a 'sweat box'), was not what I had envisaged.

'Can we open a window or get a fan from somewhere?' I asked politely

'Frack', who until now had been playing 'oily rag' to 'Frick' the 'engine driver', explained that it would 'interfere with the sound quality of the tapes'.

How the heck was I supposed to be able to answer in a clear and cogent fashion?

This was SO unfair!!!!!

I DID have a bottle of Evian with me. This was more to do with re-hydrating my petrified Champagne filled body. I was so terrified prior to this date with dismal destiny, that I had to have a 'swift glass or two' to stop me from fainting with fear.

I thought I would try and use the technique of pretending or visualizing them naked as a piglet. It was of no assistance at all, I felt positively ill!

The 'Frick' gave no quarter, she set a cracking pace.....and I did not know if it was pertinent to say: 'Whoah there possum, slow down!!!'

I was on the ropes in seconds with questions pounding my brain. An upper cut and a mighty blow followed by inside pummelling ensued. She was relentless. I stuttered and stammered. I was incapable of stringing a mere sentence or even the odd word together. This was not through a feeling of guilt, nor of trying to remember a tissue of lies. She was just so bloomin' FAST!

She took me back to the days when I was a greenhorn Norfolk lass with knockers that all the boys from miles around coveted.

Most of the questions regarding periods of employment seemed rhetorical

She merely wanted to assess how much truthfulness went into my answers.

My First job was at Jaeger, the high class clothing firm and I was (according to all the married men) top -titted -totty.

The guys in the Export office must have thought they had died and gone to nubile heaven........

I worked in the adjoining (open plan) Correspondence office and my desk was right in their line of sight.

I was a bona -fide paper shuffler and this tedium was worth £4.50 a week (daylight robbery). I remembered my very first pay packet.

It was spent with indecent girlie haste on shoes.

The only style I ever wanted was the impossibly high stilettos which glamour women from the bygone Hollywood -Age wore...the pointier the toe and the thinner the heel the better.

They looked dead kinky!!!!

My office wear was chosen from the diffusion line of the company I worked for: YOUNG JAEGER.....and it was cutting edge fashion,

I felt terribly grown up. This was Couture stuff which I could (as an employee) pick up for a fraction of the expensive going rate.

Naturally all the knitted dress I purchased got about 18" lopped off, so as to skim my 'barely out of school' buttocks.

The cashmere, or even vicuna jumpers, were skin tight and clung to my alabaster orbs and my ubiquitously erect nipples.

I didn't wear a bra (I didn't need to)....they were like twin Mount Fuji's......or, like an army, they single handed constituted an entire second front. They stood out like dog's balls.

My 'uniform' of this apparel, together with my flaxen hair and triple-decker false eyelashes (which the cat used to occasionally swat from the mantle piece), fishnet tights and stellies seemed (with hindsight) to cause quite a stir, both in and out of the office.

I was young, dumb, and full of so many lovers' cum...I would practically squelch (this was in the age of free love and pre Compulsory condoms for nookie).

The village bus would deposit my elder sister outside work in the morning, but I would stay on to get dropped off in town...and then walk BACK. Also rather than pick the bus up outside for the return journey home at 5.45...I would walk INTO town.

I often walked (actually it was more a wiggle) into town in my lunch break.

Those 3 'walks' were punctuated by a cacophony of horns and hooters (but not THOSE) of admiring drivers...I also picked up my fair share of stalkers too.

At first I was unaware of the commotion I was causing (no really)...then I started to like the attention, by the second year of my employment at this office sweat shop...I was positively THRIVING on it.

The ADULATION was brill.

Inside the office, co workers were foaming at the mouth, or so Kevin from the Export office informed me one day.

It was an unguarded moment, someone's leaving do, or a Christmas office party, and he boasted: 'We love it when you bend over your desk, we can see the crack of your arse!!!!'

I didn't wear knickers....just tights, normally black fishnets.

Apparently they had to keep tissues in their desk drawers to deal with the pre cum......

I was young and stupid and continued to encourage this kind of sniggering activity.

Then one day, one particular stalker (who I often encountered on my walks) decided to put thought into action, he came closer to me and whacked my behind with a rolled up Newspaper (probably the Eastern Daily Press)

I didn't like it and got scared.

Secondly, the men in the office were so emboldened by this idiot prick teaser (me) that they started to touch me or speak to me in a desultory and derisive manner.

The *Coup de Grace* was one lunch time as I returned to work from my 1.PM walk and a white transit full of builders drunk from their lunchtime pre- Summer Bank Holiday drink passed me.

The back doors were open...they screamed: 'COME ON BLONDIE

HOW WOULD YOU LIKE TO SUCK THIS........SIT ON MY FACE AND PEDDLE MY EARS ALL ROUND NORFOLK......'ELLO DARLIN'...... FANCY A FUCK.......YA DON'T GET MANY OF THOSE TO THE POUND......YOU FILTHY SLUT YOU KNOW YOU WANNIT......"

The reason I heard all of this was that the Bank holiday traffic made them grind to a halt a few yards from me...and they were crawling at walking pace in the SAME direction.

There was only ONE man who was strangely quiet as his other chums bayed for my quim (or whichever orifice they required)......THAT MAN WAS MY FATHER.

Ooooooooh dear: the shameful AGONY of it all. That he had to witness his workmates acting that way, and that the trollop they bayed for, was his own daughter.

I never forgot the look he gave me, and it was NEVER mentioned....but it made me realise that I was (even then) the author of my own demise.

From that day I started to act in a slightly more responsible manner.

The hemlines came down a couple of inches, my tights were changed to a more respectable opaque...and although my boobs still had a mind and movement of their own (a bra was not remotely in my lexicon of lingerie), I toned down the whole 'HELLO BOYS' caricature.

I also took control of my butt swiping stalker by growling at him to 'stay the hell out of my way'....or words to that effect. Apparently men who like to exert some kind of sexual power over a woman dislike INTENSELY a cupie doll rounding on them and spewing a torrent of vile swear words. It seemed to do the trick.

As for the Export office, I shifted my desk JUST out of their line of vision. WHAT A PRICK TEASER!

I would have traded ANY THING to be back in those days of innocence.

TOILET BREAK A DEUX

The 'interview' lumbered on. She (Ms Frick) threw cricket like curve balls and googlies. 'Frick's' mesmerising green eyes betraying when she knew she had me bang to rights, or when she thought she was uncovering a dirty little secret. She seemed disappointed that I answered 'yes' to paying Council tax.

The only mildly sticky moment was when she enquired about my TV licence.

BUGGER!!!

O.K., so that was an oversight, but, I was in fact, pure as the driven slush.

I was truly blessed. Most of my life bore scrutiny. No castles in Bonnie Scotland, no second (or third) homes in the crass Puerto Banus, or St Tropez. No Apartments on Park Lane or Park Avenue. No racehorses, sports cars, Old Masters (art wise), precious jewels----indeed no outward manifestation of a life of excess.

There was no drug habit to support, or a feckless pimp. I owed no discernable asset. No Swiss bank accounts and no off shore complicated financial shenanigans. Everything was in my name. I had no 'Nom de Guerre' where money was concerned, apart from the name that I traded under. I had spent less than 14 days out of the country on 'holiday' in the past 12 years.

I was a veritable angel.

I was beginning to read her 'poker eyes' and discern the REAL question that was being asked of me. The questions were designed to make me incriminate myself, should the whole shebang find its way to a Crown court. Even though I was a snivelling wretch as an interview virgin, I learned quickly.

'Why didn't you make a Tax return?' she asked in the manner which most of the questions were delivered: rhetorically.

'I was not aware of my tax liability' I truthfully answered.

'Why is that?' she urged.

'Well, everywhere you look, in magazines, newspapers, on TV even, you hear, or see the same phrase, over and over: 'Should prostitution be legalised?'; therefore the conclusion can be drawn that what I am doing is in fact ILLEGAL. Even some of my customers think what they are doing is wrong' I explained 'in fact, I think it makes them more excited'.

I had been told a trillion times by smug ex lawyers, accountants, judges and policemen (all punters) that 'ignorance is no defence in a court of law' and that the difference between Tax Evasion and Avoidance was 'the thickness of a prison cell wall'.

Well weren't they the smarty pants.

How very jolly. It was only 2 years previously that I had stumbled across the fact that what I was doing was, and indeed always HAD been, LEGAL. By then it was too late. I couldn't come clean now could I? It would have had the same outcome in any case surely?

I had not made the quantum leap of Legality where prostitution was concerned, with my requirement to offer a proportion of my filthy lucre to the government.

'When did you discover that you had a liability to pay tax?'

'When I received your letter' I sighed

I DESPERATELY wanted her to ask me: 'When did you first receive money for sexual favours'. That would have put a pole cat amongst the frightened pigeons.

It was a VISITING TAX INSPECTOR from another 'district' in the U.K.

That one small act (where the law is concerned) branded me a Prossie for life. Yes it's true, once you have accepted/ been paid for a night/incidence of passion (or dispassionate sex) according to the arcane statutes you are branded harlot from hell.

Yes it was merely a gift of gratitude from a very happy man, and God knows, as an employee of the Inland Revenue, he needed the excitement....... But there it was.

Then 'Frack' stepped in to ask a few questions.

'What made you think that you were somehow DIFFERENT to, say, a painter and decorator?'

I longed to say: 'I cannot actually get a few hundred flyers knocked up, with the words: REASONABLE RATES, ALL WORK CONSIDERED, NO JOB TOO BIG OR SMALL and shove them through letterboxes in my neighbourhood' I also would have relished saying: 'I cannot march along to the local Job Centre and demand a job as an Erotic Service Provider......because there wouldn't BE any---despite my experience' .

But I was mute.

There was a miasma of information to remember. There were facts and figures to impart and I simply could not remember EVERYTHING.

'What did you do when you left Jaeger then?'

'Frick'probed.

I thought back to my misspent youth, and the indignities a young 'gel' suffered in the pursuit of entertainment with the country lads..........

You would have a ride in a Ford Capri, the two drinks (Baby ham) with a handful of stale peanuts at a *local yokel* pub....and then it was down to business.

Finding a place in the great wide yonder to 'spear the bearded clam' was next on the agenda

This was what passed for 'romance' in my misspent and pent up youth.

It was the ultimate 'park and ride', but the park VENUE sometimes left a lot to be desired.

How I suffered, just to let the local lads, along with a few 'out of towners' have a 'bunk up alfresco'.

A mile from my home was a *copse* called Bell Wood. You needed to open the gate to drive into the dense and verdant thicket. It was the place I had picked primroses and violets for Mum as a child, but the attraction of flowers was dead to me now, I was a juicy adolescent and I wanted to fuck the universe. And do you know, I think I just about managed it too!!!!

If the bloke REALLY liked you he would risk the wearing down of his battery by keep the heating switched on (I couldn't enjoy myself when feeling cold) otherwise the 'fucking whilst frozen' was not for the fainthearted.

It was difficult to concentrate, because the rustle of the trees and the creaking boughs made it an eerie place to do the 'car concertina'

'I can hear people moving' I complained

'Shut up and keep bouncing on my cock' he replied in less than loving tones

'You will be CAREFUL won't you?' I pleaded in my contraception-less state

'Well, THAT'S BLOODY KILLED THE MOMENT HASN'T IT' he replied with selfish scorn.

Catholic guilt would make me console and placate the selfish prat, and we would start all over again.

The car would be awash with discarded clothes, sweat, spunk, and a tissue full of peanuts, orange slices and maraschino cherries nicked from the pub.

I whined that I could hear noises again...he ignored me...and then...THERE WAS A TAP TAP TAP on the windscreen......and there was a flashing blue light....it was the *rozzers!!!*

Oh, the eternal shame, it was the Village Bobby.

My 'lover du jour' opened the door. Mr Policeman shined his light around the interior and fixed the beam on two terrified 'copse copulators'.

'Would you mind opening the boot sir' asked Mr Plod

He hastily wrapped my frilly blouse round his bits, and did as he was told.

Duly satisfied, Mr Bobby explained: 'There has been a lot of pig theft in the area and we have had this wood under surveillance for some time, when I heard squealing I feared the worst'

'Bloody hell', I thought, 'was I screaming THAT loudly?'

He shone his torch into a face of crimson embarrassment.

'As for you young lady, don't you think you should be getting home?'
'Don't tell Mum and Dad' I pleaded.
'Just don't come here again'
And that was the end of my car fucking activities. In that wood at least...........

Norfolk was indeed a difficult place to have a love life.

My sister and I had an unhealthy interest in a very dangerous practice when we were in our teens.

Did we self abuse with sharp implements? Had we been lured into a crack den fresh from the school gates?

Did we ride without a helmet on the back of the local lad's motorbikes??

No, it was MUCH worse------

We used to hitchhike to get to dances and discos, the local lads were simply not GOOD enough for the likes of us.

The only males in our age group were delinquents, desperately inbred or ACTUAL village idiots.

No spotty *oik* was fit to finger OUR gusset.

Yes Siree, WE were going to bag at the very least, someone who lived in the NEXT VILLAGE, if not, an actual TOWN!!

We would slap on the war paint and make ourselves look 10 years older than our actual age.

Dad would look out of the corner of his eye from behind the newspaper, suck his teeth in a 'tut tut' manner and say in his lilting Irish accent: 'Sure you're not going out with all that heelball on ya (another suck of teeth) bejeezus----!!!!!!'

We ignored him. We thought he was just the silly old man that would call out to us on our departure: 'don't be late'.

'LATE'? We were lucky to get home at all.

We disappeared into swirling mists, driving rain, searing heat (in the days when we used to have summers) and gale force winds.

We were determined not to let the bloom of youth be hidden from a wider audience of yokels and bums.

We put ourselves through near death experiences (when artic lorries could not see us walking along the unlit roads).

We clambered into absolute NUTTERS' vans and we sometimes shared these varying modes of transport with all manner of livestock and pets (the one I remember most was a rabid dog).

We encountered the 'ride for a ride' mentality. I shudder when I think of it.

And, pray, for what??

To provide a country service, just like the village bus!

All we met were idiots, and those who ALSO had this 'ride for a ride' mentality, and they knew they were onto a winner, for it was the only way we could get the return journey home.

'JUST ONE MORE SUCK BEFORE WE GET YOU HOME' they would grin, and they would compound being dickheads by being moronic enough to FORCE our heads onto it (a practice which I abhor to this day).

Even if you met an acceptable bloke, there was nowhere to go, for the car was the boudoir.

How quickly one tired of the hand break popping the vertebrae one by one---or 3rd degree frostbite--because they didn't want to wear the battery down by switching the heating on----and single legs (as near as damn it, at an angle of 180 degrees) out of both wound down windows of the love-mobile.

I could have been a hell of a gymnast, Olga Korbet doing the splits on the beam?

Pa!!!! She didn't have a dick inside her at the time, though come to think of it---some of the gymnasts from the 'Eastern Bloc' were straddling the X Y chromosome distribution.

Anyway, sister did INDEED bag a Naval Aviator whilst I searched globally for my main man.

'If I look any further afield it will truly have to be called: HITCHHIKERS GUIDE TO THE GALAXY' I grimly thought.

Back in the torture chamber (interview room at the local tax office), I would have needed to be a contortionist to escape from this mess.

I was back to the original question of what I did after I left Jaeger. This was also complicated by the fact that I worked in a boutique in which I had a financial interest. I could not remember whether National insurance, or tax was paid, though I DID remember doing a second job on a factory production line, to help pay for new stock.

I had the distinct feeling she would not be remotely interested in this second job. She was leading up to the 64 million dollar baby rhetorical question. Her green eyes flashed in a 'gotcha' kind of fashion.

'And what did you do then?' she enquired

'I WORKED AT HER MAJESTY'S INSPECTOR OF TAXES'

I volunteered this information with as much disinterest as possible. So what if I did? Did that really make me a criminal master mind?

It was clear they thought it was a HUGE admission of guilt. They honestly thought I had engineered a life of peripatetic travel and financial knots that even Houdini would be unable to untie.....because of my INSIDE TAX KNOWLEDGE!

They HAD to be fucking joking!!!! Why any human being would willingly endure 3 years of dross and ennui in a work institution that smelled of boiled cabbage and pensioner's knickers was testing my power of comprehension.

I used to be so bored, I would have a power nap in the toilets after I had made the office 'afternoon tea'. Even the toilet paper was of the wipe and spread variety (IZAL) with the 'Her Majesty's Inspector of Taxes' printed on every individual sheet.

I was a mere Clerical assistant/gopher/general dogsbody. I didn't REALLY FIT IN, but in general, some of the characters, who I would describe as 'lifers' were fine.

These were human beings that had made a Faustian pact to relinquish their entire working life, from the age of 15-55------just for the financial security of a civil service pension when they were spat out into the REAL world.

To each their own, but I was not cut out to waste my life away wearing a breakfast splattered homemade cardigan and Jesus sandals for 40 years.

Had I somehow 'hurt their feelings' by rejecting the notion of a 'living death'? Was I REALLY living in a free country, where you have CHOICE employment wise? Did leaving the civil service make me a number one suspect where fraud was concerned? They obviously thought so!!!!!!

I needed a 'comfort break'. 'Frick' actually had to come with me to UNLOCK THE TOILET DOOR WHICH HAD SECRET 6 FIGURE CODE!!!!!

What was all THAT about????

If a deranged member of the public wanted to spray a hail of bullets into the Brighton Tax office, and god knows there would be multiple candidates for THAT position, then he or she would not be thwarted by security measures.

But why make this security effort for the TOILET? When I reached the inner sanctum of the cubicle I saw why they need the secret code. They had actually moved to a more luxuriant mode of mopping and wiping. The IZAL was no more. That was what I called 30 years of progress.

I assumed the loo roll had to be protected at all costs!!!

It was beyond surreal. One minute 'Frick' was assuming the role of Herr Flick to my terrified Helga. The next we are walking down the stairs to 'round two of the nail pulling torture' and being solicitous, courteous even, to one another.

'Nice weather we're having.....did your journey take long?' was the very best I could come up with.

This was their chosen profession for goodness sake!!!!

I girded up my shaking loins for the second hour of ghastly Gestapo grilling.

I wondered if they knew, or indeed CARED how they were affecting every second, minute and hour of my life.

PRICKS PATRONS AND PECUNIARY ADVANTAGES

Life goes on, no matter what.

When my dad died, I felt like shaking everyone in the universe by the collar and squealing: 'You don't understand, stop the world, because MY world has changed irrevocably'.

We live in such a secular society. We are, for the most part, unaware (or maybe we just don't care) of the tragedy and turmoil of our fellow men.

This was the case with my patrons. They could not discern from my phone manner, that I was in a world of hurt. Boy did they hear about it once they arrived!!!!

Yes, there were still 'songs to be sung and bells to be rung'. There were also cocks to be deep throated with a simultaneous licking of the gonads.

I have never lived down that 'review' left by some well meaning patron. Every visitor to my Website seemed to bypass all the other relevant information, but THIS-----they honed in and digested with relish.

Now, EVERYONE who swaggered up my well trodden stairway nursed the hope that I may do my 'party trick' in the course of the appointment.

If I ever find the bastard who left what HE thought was a compliment to my 'sword swallowing skills'…. I will take him to an area of Brighton (Dukes Mound) where he can choke on (gay, cruising) cock all bloomin' night long!

It was tough being a 'hostess with the most-est' while I was suffering with the ongoing saga of my financial history and the individuals who were hell bent on making me pay. Not for my ignorance, but for flipping them the bird in my book. Some Homo sapiens have no sense of humour.

'I bet you received your letter one day before a national Bank holiday'.

This was a comment from a lovely customer who himself was going through the hell of HMRC.

'YES, I DID…..how did you know?' I asked with a piqued interest.

We swapped verbal notes and clung to each other in desperation as the shared shit of our current lives welded us together. The act of 'Body Worship' was forgotten. This was much more cathartic for both of us.

'Yeah ruined my Christmas last year, the cunts KNOW you can't get to speak to anyone like a lawyer of anyfink' he spat.

OOooooh, the sadists! Had they no soul???

Other punters relayed similar stories. The Modus operandi had a familiar sickening thud to it.

STEAM IN HARD, MAKE THE MISCREANTS SHIT THEMSELVES, THREATEN AND HARASS THEM.

HOLD THE SODDING SWORD OF DAMOCLES, DEATH,

DESTRUCTION AND AN UNCERTAIN FUTURE OF PENURY AND BANKRUPTCY OVER THEM.

ABOVE ALL, LET THEM SWEAT.

They (HMRC) would put the brakes on, then, just as one was beginning to forget the whole fandango: WHOOSH, they would speed up and catch a resting reprobate off guard.

'They always want to interview on a THURSDAY' was another nugget of information gleaned from one of the few people I deigned to see.

'Why d'ya reckon that is?' I asked

'I got a bit jiggy with one of the female tax workers, she told me that if they could justify their existence by doing two interviews a week---then they could have a long weekend in whichever city they visited' he smiled.

Well no wonder they liked coming to Brighton for their paid jollies.

I rang my Webmaster, Noah.

'Could you make an update on my 'list of services' for me'?

He asked for the text of my addition. In all seriousness I said: 'Be bored to death by Letitcia as she regales you with tales of the unfairness of life and the slings and arrows of outrageous misfortune'

'What on earth does that mean?'

'It means, dear Noah that I have turned into the whinging wench from hell and the kind of Sex Worker that customers will gladly pay to LEAVE. I have suddenly made their home life seem more palatable'.

I was putting my patrons off. There was no point in trying to carry on.

That night, I consumed 5 times my body weight in alcohol.

Oh goodness, another fine mess I got myself into.......

We have all surely done it...woken up with the detritus of soggy chips and a half eaten big Mac, squashed by the dead weight of a drunken sot...namely ME.

If one is lucky enough not to have compounded the horror by having a 'hyena job' of a person also lying in the bed, then one can count one's blessings and move onto phase 2.

This is where it becomes apparent what mischief the alcohol addled mind has spawned.

Log on to the computer the next morning, AND THERE IT IS.

Somehow I managed to start a thread on an Australian forum--with the title: 'AUSSIE LOVERS'.

And what did I write? Well, that every Oz man (barring few exceptions) were 'woeful in the cot'

I did not NEED to be blotto to write this, but, anywho.......

To further compound this squirm making mess, I had most thoughtfully provided (what I thought was) a very becoming photo.

Big mistake.

HUGE.

Some while after my original post, the forum started questioning my parentage. The personal insults flew---and continued with one visceral comment after another.

This 'Australian Forum virgin' was rooted (no pun) to the spot, so mesmerised was I by their vitriol and spitting bile, that I started to wilfully press their hate buttons, in the form of posting yet more images for their delectation.

I was deemed by them, to be the most unattractive 'bush pig' known to their Great Okker country. It was reasoned that with my lack of ANY vestige of beauty and the fact that not only was I, in their words 'an old crone', but a seriously obese one too---that I somehow (by their reasoning) deserved a bad bedding technique.

'Thank God they don't realise that I worked in the Premiere massage parlours of Sydney' I thought--shivering inwardly.

Too late, with ever MORE mounting horror I realised that I had started YET another thread with words to that effect.

The reaction to that post was a template of the 'woeful in bed' one--by virtue of the fact that I had yet again plastered another picture of myself.

Their off kilter reasoning was predictable.

As a sex worker, that was all I deserved.

They also unkindly added that anyone who was blind enough to pay even one dollar for my dubious charms...was a dolt of the highest order.

The nastier they become, the more esoteric the pictures I uploaded.

I tried to tell them that even young beautiful nubile NON workers had almost to a woman, complained to me about the Oz man's lack of finesse and had corroborated my finding that they were metronomic pounding, 'no frills' lovers.

Hell I even devoted an entire chapter about it in my book: BODY WORSHIP.

They were sad sods of the highest order, there seemed to be only three or four active forum members (and I bet they all came from Queensland).

After a few hours one or two very gallantly came to my rescue and requested more photos or asked when I would be back in Oz, whilst another asked me to email him directly--away from the starkness of the forum.

I ignored it, but he (I ASSUMED it was a he) was persistent and I capitulated.

Several days passed when I received an email from THE SODDING AUSTRALIAN MINISTRY OF DEFENCE.

They kept it simple.

'Who are you and what is the nature of your business' was pretty much the subtext.

I had been duped. The email address which was given to me piqued my interest, because of the word: Uniform.--and that means the words: 'bull and red rag to'

What a sucker I am (no pun).

I hurriedly explained that I was not a danger to national security and that the prospect of World War 111 was not indeed a happening thing.

All this excitement was from a glass or three of bubbles.

Say what you like about me, but I am very cost and time effective.

I can have Cyber arguments with misogynistic dullards from the outback and put the country's security on a DEF CON 2 footing.

I was in enough trouble. This 'drinking to forget' business was not going to be of any comfort.

There had to be another way. If I wasn't going to, or COULDN'T work through stress, then I would try and enjoy myself with young men.

I had done research for my book and joined/signed up to a few dating sites. I would rekindle the flames and be relentless in my search for a toy boy.

I started a search and destroy mission for a cute little embryo.

DATING AND MATING WITH A RATING

One pays a severe penalty for ending up 'an old maid' who has been left on the shelf. If you are post-menopausal and living in a town where the likelihood of meeting, let alone snaring a suitable heterosexual mate is slim ….then one's prospects are like a fairy story: GRIMM!!!!

Welcome to the world of cyber dating…..when I say welcome. I mean it in a cautionary 'do not even think about it –even in one's hour of despondent desperation' kind of way!!!!

Like the sad git that I am, I found myself joining a site called 'Face Party'.

That in itself was an oxymoron (I discovered it should be renamed Bukkake Party), many remained faceless, anonymous and shielded by the internet, while wading through the hundreds (yes really) of my messages was no picnic.

I was DELUGED with approaches from piranhas sensing fresh blood.

This is a very clever Modus Operandi, in that they trick you before you have found your dating feet.

After a while it becomes apparent that NOBODY ACTUALLY WANTS TO MEET YOU, but they have a very jolly time, knacking around on their office computer with somebody stupid enough to provide them with a bit of sexual titillation.

Nice work if you can get it!!!

It also became abundantly clear that the entire male population fall foul of the 3 R's (reading, writing and arithmetic)…they cannot do ANY of these for toffee.

They blithely ignore age/geographic specification and the standard of penmanship is reduced to a caveman text patois.

One therefore receives missives from septuagenarians who reside in Mid Lothian say 'u r gr8…lets meat (sic)'

I also asked for (nay, DEMANDED) a perfect fraction: 'someone who is half my age'…..I would have made that equation A THIRD but felt it may be straying too close to 'under age' territory.

I was not kidding (young saplings are so much more malleable)…….and I caught a lot of flak for it, but that fanciful request was largely ignored.

I did state that 'limbo dancing under my age criteria will meet with disapproval'. That notion and the imaginary bar were snapped with distain across their collective burly knees.

I did receive one message which was witty and erudite:

'My eldest son is half your age but I would like the opportunity to enthral you and show you that I am an enhancer. In the event that I am not successful I will mobilise the next generation.'

As for the guys' pictures, let's say that somewhere in the U.K a distribution centre is making a financial killing renting out ARMY SURPLUS.

I know a woman loves a uniform, but this was overkill---- nearly every bugger was wearing one and posing with a phallic looking gun. No wonder we are losing the war in Iraq, there are not enough fatigues and equipment to go around because Desperate Dan of most dating sites has hired them all!!!!!

They less than flatteringly posed the 'would like a good time before I go back on tour' question

Bloomin' cheek!! The things we are meant to do for our valiant dogs of war.

I'm old enough to know when I am being shamefully manipulated, therefore the ones where they played with a fluffy kitten, 'Andrex Toilet Roll cute puppy' and worst of all, (presumably for those with a Big Ben biological clock) a borrowed toddler, got very short shrift.

One of the features of the site was the ability to see a) when someone was online or b) when a message had been read.

Of the 857 (truly) messages which found their way to my inbox (OOooer), I managed to read between the lines and discern which ones were worth a punt.

This took a considerable amount of time, but the natives got jolly restless if they felt they were not being given an IMMEDIATE reply.

'That's not very nice'.

'Ya could at least 'av let me know'.

'Yer very rude'.

'Who the f*** do ya think ya are ya stuck up bitch' were some of the more printable complaints from my 'would be' suitors, belatedly showing their TRUE nature.

I retaliated by suggesting: 'kindly remove your bovver boots from my vertebrae'----and it kind of did the trick.

Their amorous mask slipped to reveal aggression disconcertingly quickly.

I was of course a lamb to the slaughter. I stupidly replied to as many handsome hopefuls as possible....and too late, I realised that they would be content to play msn ping pong all freaking day long (don't these people WORK for a living).

This does not bode well for anyone requiring an emergency service since the police and fire dept were well represented along with the Army lads, if the uniform in the photos was to be believed.

Another feature of the site was a 'rating system' whereby the people perusing one's thoughtfully chosen images could give   the proverbial thumbs up or down.

How demoralising!!

I am proud to announce that I was adjudged to be 'HOT' (73 votes from Seeing Eye dog users) while 3 people (who will die a slow painful death) thought I was a 'DOGS DINNER'...... 3 thought I was 'BULLSH**' AND ONE KIND SOUL VOTED ME 'SLIME'!!!

I did try to join another site called Beautiful People, but no matter how airbrushed my submitted pictures (I tried 5 times) I was rejected for age/looks related reasons.

So many dating sites have this beauty fascism built into the agenda. HOT OR NOT (which rates me 8 out of 10) or GORGEOUS NETWORKS who have a similar ratio of morons that this 'sorry love you're not my type' mentality is enough to make hermits and recluses of those who are not Kate bleedin' Moss.

Even my beautician ('work harder luv' I hear you cry)....WAS TOLD THAT BECAUSE SHE WAS OVER THE HILL AND OVERWEIGHT, that she would have to pay a larger premium, as she would be 'difficult to place'.

Frankly my bible reading classes, macramé and knitting lessons and budgie (oh, all right...maybe a cat for my lap as well) seemed to beckon.

I DID HOPE THAT THE EMBRYONIC FIREMAN WOULD GET IN TOUCH THOUGH. And by Jove, and golly gosh, he DID------

All the signs were good. He rang to say he would be 10 mins late (good boy).

Though already I thought that it was slightly tiresome that his mobile was: a) out of order b) been nicked c) out of credit (due to the fact that he did not now have a job), and therefore he had to go to a phone box to close the final details of my address.

So, the death knell of my buzzer rang eventually.

He was as advertised (from a dating site) 6'4", cute and with size 13 *Timberlands*---and we all know what THAT means don't we ladies?

'I see you arrived empty handed' I said

'Wot, you though' I wus gonna come wiv me overnight didya' he replied

This is where you know the age gap cannot be bridged.

Sure older women fancy younger men and vice versa---but would it be SSssssooooomuch trouble for them to have by passed the JERK phase???

I had ensured fresh flowers, alcohol---and fluffy towels were available, and he, in is youthful arrogance had just rocked up.

I was supposed to be grateful.

Within another 5 minutes his first brain numbingly gauche statement tumbled from his lips like a Pyrenean avalanche: 'Yeah, your-- like ---similar age to me Mum, --------ME MUM LOOKS YOUNGER THOUGH.

Resisting the urge to head butt him, I smiled sweetly as he slowly but surely hanged his self-importance with the misplaced swagger of the barely post pubescent.

'Wotcha pay for this then' he asked, surveying the view and opulent surroundings

I declined to answer.

'I reckon on a scale of 1 to 10, I'm 9 an'half' he beamed.

(Gee, wasn't I just the lucky little possum)

I declined to comment on that too

Soon he was making the worst kind of social gaffe (where you are actually looking to get laid) every 5 minutes.

'Is that a hair on yer boob?' he asked

I couldn't see one, but he persisted: 'yeah, it IS' he exclaimed holding the 'ducks down' of a blond hair (which MOST women have on their breasts) between his thumb and forefinger.

"Ere, yer not a bloke are ya??' he exclaimed.

Through gritted teeth I assured him I wasn't.

Stumbling on through this less than torrid date, we reached a stroking, touching hands thing on my leather lounge.

'Ow much longer have I got to keep doin' this for?' he whined.

If this young buck wanted pulverised knackers, he was going the right way about it.

He then proceeded to lecture: 'Ya didn' make it plain wot it was you wuz lookin' for in yer ad'.

In short he wanted a zip less fuck within 30 seconds of arrival, hell, even my PATRONS DON'T WANT (or get) THAT.

He simply wanted a hole, a vagina on legs.

This was not a happening thing.

I questioned his M.O and his answer was: 'Yeah but you only do THAT kind of soft lovey dovey (stroking and caressing) stuff with someone you luv an' care abart'.

This dating young 'bucks' was a bad idea. I would have to face my demons and try to help myself come to terms with the enormity of the situation.

Even a less that charitable acquaintance said: 'It's no less than you deserve'

It was back to the drawing board.

And that board said: BRACE YOURSELF SHEILA.

RIMMING THE REVENUE

'Frick' and me, reconvened in the stifling sweat box after our comfort break. I wondered what my 'whore whisperer' had found to talk about in the way of appalling small talk to 'Frack'.

We had to do 'part two' of the toe curling official ceremony, with an assurance that we 'had not discussed the case' on my loo lull.

Under any other circumstances, I would have joked and been at my jocular best.

But I had to play it straight. We were back to debating the vicissitudes of legality, morality and liability.

It is one thing to find that what you are doing is perfectly legal. However, with prostitution, nothing is as clear cut as the 'quid pro quo' between client and service provider.

My mate Kei once told me how he nearly soiled his boxer shorts when at a licensing hearing, he was asked under what circumstances he would be bound (law wise) to refuse drink to customers in his watering hole.

'If the patron was under age' he answered correctly

'If the patron was already noticeably intoxicated' was his second correct answer.

There was a pause, the person who had the power to giveth or take away his licence, lunged forward and hissed 'If the person is a KNOWN PROSTITUTE!'

Poor Kei. We were very close.

I not only held my book launch at his glorious hotel, I drank in another of his establishments: Brighton Rocks. I therefore always made a joke of standing in the doorway, and shouting at the top my voice: 'Are you serving prostitutes today?'

They were such quick witted smart arses, they would shout back: 'Sold out I'm afraid.....got the Dover Sole though!!'

That was only ONE of the toe curling stupid laws that I encountered in my daily life. The others were: 1) standing on the side of the road for longer than a nano- second waiting for a taxi (could be deemed as street walking/touting), 2) calling to any mates who happened to be driving by (ditto) 3) being in the least bit friendly to ANYONE. They were all technically no -go -areas.

We were social pariahs, beleaguered, misunderstood, frowned upon AND STILL HMRC wanted our money.

The interview limped along. They were talking about stuff which related back to 1981!!!! I had been told that they were within their power to go back to 1945, and sought solace in the fact that I was not born until 7 years later!

Ha, that was a silver lining!!!!

'Frick' at one point showed me a figure she had written on a piece of paper. Crikey!!! There were a lot of noughts. If that was their idea of my liability, then I would be 'gum rubbing gonads' as an octogenarian.

She pointed to a page from my Web -Site, it contained the prices and list of services I provided. 'Are they your prices?' she asked. 'Yes' I responded with a knowing grin 'but I'm thinking of putting them up'

This tickled her for some reason. Well I'm glad SHE thought it was funny.

Suddenly, my torment (for this day at least) was over.

'I will be contacting your accountant to see how you arrived at THESE figures' she spat 'and then we will decide if we will require another interview'

I remembered the line from G.I Jane, where Demi Moore's character beseeches her commanding officer: 'BUT I CAN'T GO THROUGH THIS SHIT AGAIN!!!!'

With as much dignity as a broken woman can muster, I wrapped my Pashmina around my trembling shoulders, shook hands with my interrogators (what a hypocrite) in a jolly 'nice to see you, we must do this again, drive carefully' fashion, and with the 'Whore whisperer' leading, my 'pelvis had cleared the building'

We had a post-mortem prior to his departure back to London. He thought I 'did well'.

I disagreed.

I felt I kissed ass due to lack of knowledge, I felt I leaned FORWARD in my seat in a pathetic attempt to show co-operation, I felt I lost the command of King's English through sophisticated interviewing tactics, I felt that I was doing EVERYTHING in my power to help.

This was to no avail.

I was disempowered.

I was a snivelling wretch searching for the merest hint of kindness, the embodiment of a pleading refugee and as pathetic as a participant in a war where the other side held all the weapons----and where the rules stated there could be no fighting back.

I hated everything about my powerless role.

They had done this gig a zillion heart aching times before. My brief must have been bored 'beyond relief' at the parochial/small time nature of the enquiry. He was used to high powered cases where multi- millions of defrauded money was at stake. I am my worst critic and I thought I sucked.

To this end I decided I would have to toughen up.

This is what Letitcia did next...........

TREADING THE BOARDS WITH DIVA STRINE

I put on a stage show, and I did it standing up as well!!!!!!

I was asked the previous October if I would care to talk passionately about any subject dear to my heart. This was the premise for an evening called 'The Catalyst Club'

The venue was at a comedy playhouse and I decided naturally to talk about Sex.

I talked, or should that read: seethed and railed with indignation, about the futility of searching for a Male escort, or indeed ANY Male Escort who was not emotionally wedded to his cock. I was certain the subject matter would appeal to both men and women regardless of their sexual orientation.

My intro music was a resounding rendition of the A/C D/C classic: 'Whole Lotta Rosie' and I provided a slide show of myself in a dizzying array of costumes, hats and glasses which serve as images on my website: Brighton Body Worship.

I wanted to whip then into an opening frenzy, and hoped the delivery of my show would get the laughs in all the right places. I had NEVER done a cock-a-mammie- crazy thing like it in my life, but I'm game for a laugh (along with my patrons who get to see me naked) and up for a challenge and wanted to prove (to myself) that I wasn't a wimp.

It was undoubtedly the hardest, most heart stopping act of madness, I had ever voluntarily done. It took three days for the pains of stress in my chest to subside and I swore I would never do it again

Naturally when they asked me back to do a stint in conjunction with (Festival of age), a celebration of the elder stateswomen of certain professions, I heard the voice of 'no reason whatsoever' say: 'yes'.

My mate 'Harry the Actor' was drafted in to help me hone my show. He was a remarkable character who always had the ability to make me laugh and think in equal measure.

I played a heinous trick on him once, just to strike at the very heart of his Spanish machismo.

I love a practical joke...so when he was crowing about his sexual prowess and his ability to impregnate his gorgeous partner Tracy (with certainty) ON HIS FIRST ATTEMPT, something had to be done.............

I was lucky enough to be in collusion with the fun loving Tracy----who thought it would be good for a giggle, and she gave me all the ammunition I needed.

This was going to be a great 'sting'

He had boasted to anybody that cared to listen, within a 5 mile radius: -

'yeah, I reckon my sperm is Turbo charged. It is Super sperm'.

He was due to go on holiday to see his ma and pa abroad---and to tell them that (according to the pathologists) they could be grandparents once more.

Tracy showed me the test results from the laboratory---so I had the advantage of technical jargon with which to reel him to his impotent demise. What little minxes!!!!!

Timing is everything and I decided to be the bearer of bad news ONE day before he was jetting off to boast of his industrial strength baby batter.

I'm not the best impersonator in the world (I decided to bring his macho world crashing around his penile prowess via phone) but I do a pretty nifty Irish accent.

I raised it a few octaves to *Mrs Doubtfire* type proportions.

'Allo!!!' barked Harry (he doesn't 'answer' a phone---he snaps at it like it's annoying him in the middle of knitting a scarf).

'OOOoooo, would that be Mr Jones?'

"Yep' he snarled guardedly.

'This is terribly embarrassing-----I'm sorry to have to inform you-----you DID have a sperm test on the 15th Feb did you not?'

Suddenly I had his attention, and I detected the smell of fear down the telephone wire. He rapidly switched the background music off so he could hear one of his best mates conning him.

'Yeah, I think it was on that day---is there a problem?' he snapped

'Well, now let me see----it's just that there were TWO Mr Jones in the laboratory that day----and I know it's bad luck but the initials were almost the same------and somehow the results got switched------'

I scrunched my fist into the quavering hole that was my mirthful mouth. Delicious!!!!

'What a' yer sayin???' demanded a not so cock sure Harry.

'Now dear---I know you are upset---and I don't know how the mix up occurred---but your results indicate a low---indeed scant presence of sperm at all!!!!!'

I swear I heard his gonads drop. I thought he took it pretty well bearing in mind that he had gone from hero to zero in the time it takes to say the word 'wank'

He said he was going on holiday, and that he would reschedule when he got back. He sounded crestfallen.

I suddenly felt guilty and I couldn't let him suffer for an entire 8 days.

I gave him a few hours of agony and then decided to go and visit him in his retail emporium.

He was ASHEN FACED.

'What's up?' I rhetorically asked.

He tried to act casually---but I knew the fear he was hiding.

There is only one thing worse than being called a dud fuck----and that is an impotent one.

His very 'raison d'etre' was in question.

I patiently let him relate the story, bade him a good trip and counselled him not to 'worry too much'.

As I walked out I said, (IN MY RICHEST 'ORISH ACCENT): 'Fancy having a scant presence of sperm.'

I was 200 yards up the street before I heard the most disgraceful barrage of profanity.

Mission: 'kick a man in the nuts' was accomplished!!!

Harry helped me with the delivery for my forthcoming stage show. I don't know why they had asked me back.

My name was allegedly 'put forward', but I felt I wanted names addresses and current medical records of the sadists involved.

I was 'on' before Diva. (Name has been changed but let us see if you can recognise U.K's stage sweetheart).

What a nasty, miserable, ungracious, batty drunken bitch. She snarled/snapped at me to 'shut up' as I quietly whispered to my mates in the corner as she did her sound check.

Comediennes are most unfunny in real life.

The promoter and flunkies were abasing themselves and slinging themselves at her feet while I was left to my nervous devices.

The promoter then sidled up and said: 'Letitcia, can you tone it down a bit???'

WHAT THE ****

'You mean my bloomin' material?' I spluttered.

'No, your intro music'....he surveyed the room...'might be too much for this lot'

So a pounding: 'Gimme some lovin' by Steve Winwood, had to be muted affair, all in the name of keeping the 'entourage' and the weird audience happy.

This was going to be like putting Guns and Roses on before the Philharmonic Orchestra.

It was going to be unimaginably awful.

I saw the 'audience' arrive and knew in a sinking stinking heartbeat it was never going to fly.

If the League of Gentlemen ever collided with the contents of a (elderly) GAY 'ye olde Music hall' ----------this was my fresh hell.

All the effort to find the right lines, the knowing inflections and the bursting pregnant pauses---were lost when I saw the size of the mountain I was being asked to scale.

They would NEVER warm to material about a 70 year old been taken up the 'wrong 'un' would they (well it WAS the festival of age)????

IT WAS A FREAKING NIGHTMARE.

The final humiliation was yet to come.

Ms Diva and Pianist had a tight schedule (for hot cocoa and an early night perhaps)....and the promoter/milquetoast sidled up yet again, AS I WAS STILL PERFORMING and whispered: 'could you wrap it up...'cos she's gotta get on'

I mean BLISTERING BOLLOCKS AND BURNT BUMS...how DISMISSIVE!!!

I had to cut short my account of deflowering a fuzzy peach skinned virgin. My 'Big Finish' was ruined by Age concern.

I rang the 'promoter' 7 MOTHER MUNCHING TIMES, to enquire: 'what in the name of Basil Brush's butt was you THINKING??? Is there a particular reason why you would put me through being publicly dismantled?'

He cowered somewhere I think, since he did not return my calls (Bastard), and I vowed not to rest until his cheeky countenance showed naked fear when confronted with a woman on the edge.

'Oh well Letitcia', a mate opined 'THAT'S SHOW BUSINESS'.................

It was not the 'toughening exercise' I had hoped for and I was cast adrift once more to face the daily tedious tax torment of what was to become of me.

Finally, just as I was beginning to forget about my troubles, there was word that they were coming to see my 'Bed Sheet' man, AND that they wanted to see me several weeks after that very meeting.

Just to make life interesting, they issued the directive that they would like my accounts to 'be agreed' by the time of my next assignation with them. How in hell was I going to do that??

If they were not enthused by my £4000 claim for Male prostitutes in the name of research, how was I going to negotiate the rest?

HOT FOR TEACHER

Grammar school was for me, an arduous affair.

It was impossible to concentrate on learning, when my libido was bungee jumping. My horny hormones were in a minx like maelstrom and my attention was diverted to either the mud splattered 6th formers (I went for the older man in those days) or teachers both male and female.

The hottest of all was the delectable MR PLUM.

He taught History, but us young gels didn't give a stuff about The Great Fire, Guy Fawkes or The Crimea, all we knew was, when we had (whoopppeeee!!) a double class of History, our navy blue knickers were so moist with adolescent excitement, we practically had to wipe the seat with our the embroidered hankies (the only time grandma's Christmas present came in useful).

The man was a shambles. He had the gait of Herman Munster and the dress sense of......well... a Historian, meaning: NONE AT ALL.

He wore the same bottle green, oversized, hand knitted (by his missus we found out) jumper. It was going baggy at the hem and there were one or two stitches which needed a touch of 'knit one' and 'pearling two'.

His shoes were a highly burnished antique brown aubergine, and they were so old (yet beautifully preserved) they squeaked and creaked as he strode into class.

I cannot remember the style of his hair, but he continually touched it and swept his hand through it distractedly. Fuck, he was driving us girlies CRAZY!!!

It was JET BLACK.

His eyes were the kindest and most compassionate limpid pools of 'yumscrumptiousness' (barring baby seals and Bambi), and I longed to bathe and luxuriate in them as his favourite pupil.

Any modern razor would find his stubble rising up a nano second after the sweep of a triple blade. He had a permanent brutish and thug like shadow. We longed for him to crush our delicate schoolgirl faces with his inbuilt 'please grater', we would have worn our bruised lips and facial rashes as a badge of pride and a *'rite de passage'*

And, oh, roger me sideways with a banana: those rosebud lips. They soared and dipped with alarming aesthetic beauty. He licked them all the time and when he SPOKE...we all collectively keeled over with the honey/treacle/warmth effect.

His manner of speech was so soft and shy that we yearned to do well in our studies to make him more confident.

HE WAS SOOOOOO SHY!!!!

HE DIDN'T REALISE HOW BLOODY GOOD LOOKING HE WAS. And that was a killer combination.

My best mate Beverly used to purposely unbutton her summer uniform so that he could get a REAL good look. She was wasting her time, for he seemed oblivious to the dreamy far away look that the female of the class wore.

We worshipped him.

He was a 6' 5" (oh yes.....he was a tall mother fucker) he was everything we wanted: TALL, DARK, HANDSOME, AND OBLIVIOUS TO THE FACT.

We would have drunk his bath water, loved him in sickness and health or SHARED him, if only it meant we could get close to him for a short while.

There was only 2 ways to ensnare him: TO BE A TOP PUPIL AND GET COPIOUS GOLD STARS----OR BE CRAP AND REQUIRE EXTRA TUITION.

I took the second route and was catatonic when he came so close I could smell his SOAP (it was Life Bouy).

He would put one arm on my desk, and the cuff of his 'Grandad shirt' would ride up to reveal the blackest shiniest and softest hairs creeping out of the pristine whiteness of his sleeve.

His whole body seemed to ENVELOP my 13 yr old frame in a gorgeous carapace. I was in a world of deep 'smit' and I was about to freaking well EXPLODE!!

If I did not find something to stick up my school girl vagina, I was going to bloody well SELF COMBUST.

I think most fondly of the padded, satin (and suspiciously stained) covered coat hanger whenever I visit home, since that was what I used as a substitute for my unrequited History Hysteria.

Oh Mr Plum, you were a beautiful hunk of manhood!!!!!

In contrast there was Mrs Smith. A plain surname indeed, for an exceedingly plain and ugly woman. She was a hateful harridan and a crap teacher.

I wish I had paid more attention. She would drone on about logarithms and Binary numbers. And as for the 'PYE' equation, what earthly good was it going to be in 'real life'?

I resented having to bend my nubile mind to the 'if a man is given 7 apples every 6 miles that he walks, how many will he have if he walks for half an hour with a friend at 2mph????'

I now needed that knowledge to provide figures to Bed Sheet.

There is little point to employing an accountant if he cannot make legitimate 'tax deduction' claims. For this, he needed me to number crunch my way through four years' worth of Patrons. It was almost as painful as the four year's toil and trouble.

It came to me as a considerable surprise, that I had seen way over quadruple digits in the Body worship stakes and was glad that the freeholder did not contact me for renewal of a threadbare stair carpet. I had to convert that figure into money spent per client.

I mentally went through the well-oiled machine (no, NOT the vibrator) of 'HELLO' to 'AU REVOIR' in my Body Worship appointments

This was my blueprint: The intercom buzzes and it's a quick squirt of air freshener for the inner vestibule (not THAT one).

The willing victim comes to the door to be greeted by a warm bear hug and offer of libation or more. He is invited to sit and enjoy both the view of Brighton Pier and his sexily attired hand maiden, who is scudding around the kitchen talking a load of complete tosh and testicles.

He admires my art collection and looks at my cornices and high ceiling. Soft music plays and while 'enjoying his service' he can elect for silence, classical or make your ears bleed thumping rock/metal.

We go to 'phase two' (the boudoir), with a pause on the way for the loo (for him), where fluffy towels and pristine toilet bowl await.

Into the inner sanctum, with sumptuous decor and the usual paraphernalia is on hand for any sudden request.

Baby wipes, tissues and tongue fresheners (mint and spearmint) are used with impunity.

Having had the seeing to of his natural born life, he pauses to pay the bathroom another visit, pays a King's ransom and bids a farewell.

THIS NEVER WAVERS. I had to convert this to the cash that I had spent. Mrs Smith you miserable old crone, where was you now????

This was only one of the aspects of money spent on the business. The major expenditure was ME.

I emailed Bed Sheet: 'These are the figures for my beauty expenditure, over and above what I would normally spend.

'Blimey' I continued, 'for this kind of money I should look like Claudia bleedin' Schiffer'

He didn't reply.

I longed for a good old belly laugh, and wistfully thought of Bruce, who arrived on a Singapore Airlines 747 just one year before...........

A NAUGHTY 'ICKLE SCHOOLBOY

I sat in a restaurant/bar with a view overlooking the sea and the Brighton Pier.

Tears were streaming down my face.......

They were however, tears of great hilarity.

Oh how my sides ached.

Bruce was his name, and he was my weekly patron (regular as clockwork), at one of the largest and best 'cathouses' in Sydney.

When I left to go on my travels, and to eventually return to the U.K, he was obviously 'left in the lurch'.

We did however stay in touch. He was very kind to me in a number of ways, and I was very happy to see him again after an absence of ELEVEN YEARS.

Since that time, Bruce had not been inside a woman (maybe the Statue of Liberty....but that doesn't count!!)

Now, in that time, my working practices had segued for various reasons to the point that I DID NOT OFFER SERVICES OF A PENETRATIONAL NATURE.

It had not escaped my notice that I had been castigated for that, by of all people---- fellow service providers----like they didn't have the bloody *CHOICE.*

'Body Worship' had been honed to such a point (or skill) which ever way you want to view it, that it seemed no longer necessary and indeed was hardly EVER asked for.

My dilemma was: DO I TELL HIM BEFORE HE STARTS THE 13,000 MILE ARDUOUS JOURNEY FROM OZ???????

I decided to wing it, though several of my good mates were appalled at my treachery: "You mean he's coming all that way, after all this time----and you're not even going to FUCK him?" they screamed.

I admit this line of reasoning did rather tickle my chuckle muscle---to the point that I self-combusted with laughter whenever I thought of this conundrum.

He arrived, and over a convivial lunch, related the difficulty he had in finding an adequate *'replacement'* after my departure.

Bruce was pedantic regarding personal hygiene/cleanliness/diet and exercise. I mean, his underpants alone were starched and bleached to the most brilliant of white, which is why I found his account of looking for comfort most amusing

He sought succour in the arms of: A CHUFFING STREET CRACK HEAD!!!!!

She was apparently 19, with a voluptuous hour glass figure and tumbling raven coloured hair. This and the full ruby lips sealed his fate.

She didn't actually have anywhere to take him for his pleasure, and he found himself in the back of a dirty magazine shop in Darlinghurst Road. In effect it was a 'wanking room' for the soiled raincoat brigade.

He paid her the money----AND SHE LEFT TO GET A FIX.

My poor Bruce was left in a cum splattered cubicle with the detritus of 'fisting' and 'doggie' mags, together with the odd foil or stray needle.

Upon her return she disregarded dearest 'clean freak' and anally retentive Bruce, AND PROCEEDED TO JACK UP complete with tourniquet.

As if this wasn't bad enough, she bought back an Aussie staple. No, NOT a can of Recsh's Beer (brewed and ONLY found in N.S.W), NOT a Violet Crumble (like a Crunchie bar)--nor a 'sanger sarnie' (sausage sandwich), A VANILLA SLICE.

This culinary treasure was basically COLD CUSTARD BETWEEN FLAKY PASTRY DUSTED WITH ICING SUGAR.

It's was real messy!!!

She shoved the needle in her arm and the pastry between her scarlet lips--AND SIMULTANEOUSLY grabbed the dick of what must have been a mortified/terrified ex patron of yours truly.

My belly simply ACHED with mirth and merriment....and what was making me giggle even more was, after hearing this account of a disastrous coupling, did I confess that after 11 years and a not inconsiderable distance...THAT HE STILL WOULD NOT BE RAM RAIDING DOGGY FASHION.

Having mopped my tears (I truly have never laughed so much) we made a date for the next day.

'No worries,' as they say in Oz-----guess what, HIS PREFERENCES HAD CHANGED TOO.

Life is full of surprises, as I was only too aware. I decided to live each day as if it were my last, just like the lads and lasses in war torn Britain. The upside was that I could not get pregnant, and didn't CARE about getting fat. I gorged on life and went into semi-retirement.

'There's no point to working any more Harry' I moaned one day.

'How do you mean?'

'Well, the fourth suck is always going to be for Gordon Brown, so it kind of takes the FRISSON out of cock sucking'.

LADIES THAT LAUNCH

When you write a book, and therefore, when you are put on some arcane media LIST, all notion of a quiet night in with comfortable pyjamas and hot cocoa are flung into the English Channel.

If you have a 'P.R' agent, this problem is solved by the sweet words: 'they will PAY an appearance fee'

If not, and in Brighton they want EVERYTHING for nothing---you are cruising for a bruising.

I went to the openings of envelopes as a 'Z' list wannabe, assented to a dizzying array of interviews and photographic shoots and learned, out of nowhere, completely new crafts.

The 'double kiss greeting' taught me to fix my different hats with sturdy grips. The manhandling by over eager sycophants reminded me of the Queen Mother's silent edict 'don't touch the exhibits'.

I become nauseatingly ubiquitous and was referred to as: 'That bloody Letitcia woman' I wanted to become well known if it killed me----and it was killing me softly. The sales of my book may have depended on it, but the price was stratospheric.

I honed my newly acquired persona: as an all smiling, all sincere game show host on a bus man's holiday.

Once was a curiosity, twice was indulgence and by the third time of meeting the same regurgitated people and photographers, holding the same warm sponsored wine, and smelling the rotting stench of putrefied garlic and smoker's breath........it was a sorry ass joke.

As for guest spots on the radio, these were merely public ambushes.

Southern Counties: The Sarah Gorrell show was the gladiatorial arena, and at 7.AM, I was not best prepared for the onslaught, especially the cheeky little question: 'Do you pay tax?'

'You know' I responded 'government cannot have it both ways---with no pun intended Sarah.'

Now I saw they could have it in as many positions as they liked. Bareback even!!

The TV production companies were the very worst offenders in the use and abuse stakes..........

The Tricia Goddard Show was a case in point.

After a furious ping pong of phone conversations, I read the email which said:

'I would like to confirm that the Tricia Goddard Programme will book you for an interview, this will be for Townhouse TV, and it will appear on Channel 5.....

Well, 'whooopy do' you may think.....

WRONG.

Here follows an email that I sent to the producers.......TWO DAYS before airing!!!

'Greetings, to say I was somewhat perplexed and bemused by the outcome of the telephone conversation with **** yesterday, would be an understatement too far.

I admire her bravery.....it could not have been an easy call to make.

To segue from what I (erroneously) assumed would be something even remotely and tenuously linked to the sex industry, into non-existent family disputes----words (for once) fail me.

As I said to the researcher: 'Are you kidding me or what?

I have no way of knowing if this was your intention all along, or whether the planned show fell through. ***Authors Note***I know what I ****ing well think!!!!!

I was nonplussed to be asked to provide a family member (who would supposedly not agree with what I was doing)

From the lengthy conversations I have had both with yourself and ***** you both know only too well this is NOT the case, and I would NEVER be complicit in trying to provide that----simply to make an appearance on the 'goggle box'!!

Then to be asked (at 48 hrs notice) to provide some or (in your desperation, ANY, various people from the sex industry was somewhat insulting.

Had I been given enough time (our original communication was aeons ago), I can think of some cracking characters who could have provided lively debate.

But then, these same people would not want to be misrepresented and manipulated.

I think the general public got wise to this with the Vanessa Feltz debacle.... ****I should have put EXPOSE******

I may not be stupid but I am ignorant and naive with regards to Television. Not any more though!!!!!

It has been an expensive lesson.

I will swallow my not inconsiderable loss of earnings along with feeling like a chuffing idiot.

Regards

Letitcia: Erotic Service Provider, and author of the book BODY WORSHIP'.

They laughably contacted me AGAIN some months down the 'use and abuse wannabe' help line. I must have been filed under the heading: 'Dullard who hasn't the foggiest about the vicious world of television'.

I related the Dogs dinner of the past disaster, they offered a derisory

£200 for my trouble (which had never been paid), and then proceeded to do the same thing again.

I realised why nice guys finished last (even where orgasms are concerned.) concluding that, if you give a second chance to the bad guys----they have carte blanch to do it again.

Representatives of the Jeremy Kyle Show (Manchester based!!), some oleaginous spit balls from Endemol TV who bitch pumped me shamelessly for information, Kerrang! Radio (based in Birmingham) and the Sharon Osborne Show, all gave me a bell, wasted my time and eventually showed themselves as soulless charlatans.

No matter, I soldiered on. March or die has always been my feeling where life's rich tapestry was concerned. The fact that I felt it was a tatty threadbare rug was immaterial.

Then a burning bush (and I've had a few of those in my time) offered me another life line.

I was nominated as 'Favourite scene personality'---for a GAY MAGAZINE, and asked to present' prizes for The Golden Handbags: The Gay Oscars.

I bumped into the unsuspecting Mayor of Brighton.

'I would shake hands but I appear to have my hands full', I gushed

'If I come any closer then so will mine' was his Worshipful's reply.

'I would love you to interview me' twinkled Brighton's 'King of Bling'.

I did not realise the mayhem that ensued at City Hall, my intended interviewee did not know of my Sex Worker Status (I was introduced as a writer), but somehow, the meeting of diametrically opposed minds went ahead.

This was unfamiliar territory, frightening—and exciting.

The Mayoress was in attendance, lest I reverted to the Nympho nuances that are thought to be the trademark of all prostitutes.

It was so enjoyable,

I continued to seek out high profile members of the community with whom to dish the dirt and have an irreverent giggle. It was liberating and energising, with no sexual favours being used as a safety net.

Wonderful!!!

These journalistic pieces of frivolity saved me from 'the endless circuit' and I was reborn.

My second date with 'Frick and Frack' loomed, and I felt I didn't give a rancid rat's rump.

FIRM AND FULL OF SPERM

'Life is what happens when other people are making plans'. I tended to agree with John Lennon, and to that end, I became nostalgic for a happier time and the places and people I had met on my travels, rather than worry about financial and litigation meltdown.

A travel programme showed the thoroughfare of Pitt Street in Sydney and I thought back to surreal times, especially at the Hilton Hotel..............

I have stared down the barrel of a shotgun twice in my action packed life time. Once quite literally and the second time metaphorically----but both incidences were equally scary.

The first incident with a twelve bore shotgun was when I was on an 'Out call' in a leafy hamlet where the very rich or retired play out their 'golden years' in sumptuous gracious living.

This residence had a full time gardener, House keeper, Game keeper....but unlike certain members of the Royal family, the Master of the house was not only able to squeeze his own toothpaste but just about his own trigger.

I was STARVING, and after a quick dip in his Olympic size pool and a relaxing pre dinner Gin and Tonic in the Cabana/Gazebo (told you it was posh)...I was ready to chow down.

My 'Date' took the deliciously prepared food from the Aga Cooker and I took up my place at the kitchen table

'I could eat the crutch out of a rag doll Jonathan' I moaned 'and half the pubes as well'

With a plate piled high of the finest meat and vegetables money could grow (they all came from the vast estate), and a traditional toast of: 'I WONDER WHAT THE POOR PEOPLE ARE DOING NOW?' I proceeded to attack my repast with considerable relish.

My fork was halfway between plate and pout when the back door was kicked in------BY HIS ESTRANGED WIFE.

Jon jumped up like a scalded cat and she looked me over with a superior sneer.

'So, my dear' she said to 'you are the new tart now?'

I didn't reply and wondered what on earth my paying protector was doing, for he seemed to have disappeared altogether. What a bounder!!

She continued: 'Don't look so surprised my dear, there have been many others before you----but I must say they didn't look as cheap'.

I didn't look as cheap as her shot, especially as my 'get up' of leather/rubber was at my Client's request.

Withering comments are par for the course where a deposed wife is concerned and I took my verbal abuse in silent stoicism. My Fork still hovered, waiting for a small break in the unimaginable horror of the proceedings. 'If I could have just ONE nibble of my home reared lamb cutlet I would gladly (if needs be) have a catfight with this disgruntled lady' I thought.

The husband and wife team had much in common, for at this moment Jon made a welcome appearance----by kicking in the KITCHEN door. Yes, where door kicking was concerned they were compatible with a capitol C.

My relief turned to consternation when I saw what he was carrying, and more worrying was the look of 'Mr diminished responsibility'.

He raised a gun in the general direction of his Missus, and the cold steel of the barrel paled in significance to his wild narrowing eyes. I had seldom seen such visceral hatred.

Cue 'er indoors for a spot of histrionics: 'Yes, kill me why don't you Jonny......KILL ME, I have NOTHING left to live for. Do it now why don't you'.

Since I was pretty much between shootER and shootEE, and I fervently wished she would shut the fuck up.

He continued with his weird unblinking stare until I could bear it no longer. I had signed up for: SWIM, SUPPER, SUCK......but not SLAUGHTER on a Charles Manson type scale. I stood up very gingerly and said: 'If my fee is in the normal place Jon, and if it is all the same to you I would really prefer at this juncture, to leave'

I high tailed it out of Dodge City and vowed never to do another outcall. I would become the ultimate interior control freak.

But then, a Letitcia vow carries the weight of the male lie: 'no, I won't come in your mouth'

Therefore, when I heard the edict: 'Letitcia, you have a 4 hours booking at the Hilton....we will ring a cab for you now'.....I jumped to attention.

Damn!!!.....I really HATED outcalls, you never knew if the entire Paramatta footie team was hiding in the bathroom ready to pounce.

It was with a heavy heart that I set off to my imagined doom......

Pitt St, Sydney, up the long ramp to the grey monolithic structure which was Sydney Hilton International, up the escalators, past the reception where they give you the gimlet eye (or is it my imagination)........turn right to the lifts (pays to know where they are)...and to the penthouse (good sign).

When I say: HUBBA HUBBA HUBBA, you will know what I mean.

What a vision!! He looked like the winner of the annual Aussie Iron Man competition....the epitome of physical wholesomeness and triathlete honed athleticism....and his manners were implausibly (for an Aussie male) impeccable.

'Please come in, can I get you some Champagne, I bought you a present

73

(beautifully wrapped chocolates with a posy of flowers), take a seat and make yourself comfortable, ...kick your shoes off, wow they are high, would you like a foot massage?' (Though in his own strangled accent).

These are the times when you ponder: 'Why would anyone covet a white collar 9-5 job?'

Now normally upon arrival at a hotel escort job, the first thing to do is:

a) ask to use the bathroom (so you can see the entire Aussie Rules Squad are not waiting to spit roast you), and then, ring back to base to let them know everything is ok...and that the job can commence from that time forward.

I was in flagrant breach of the prossie protocol since I was having such a spiffing time.

'Ken aye git youse a strawb to sling in thet possum' he asked in his broad Queenslander accent......

He most certainly could cobber, and we had a glass or three before the phone rang.

It was the Parlour wondering what had happened to me. I assured them everything was okay and went into phase two of the well-oiled *Modus*: 'May I use your bathroom please?'

'Are youse sure yer don' wanna tinkle on ma tonsils bubbalah?' my cheeky dream date enquired.

I assured him the conventional method suited me just fine.

BUT THERE IT WAS: Every cream, every perfume, lotion, potion and accoutrement....that a self-respecting, rich WOMAN would wear.

BOLLOCKS!!!!

It could mean only two things.

I wasn't going to see my unborn children in his cornflower blue eyes....and there was an unspecified 'Sheila' around.

'Er, I hate to beg the question....but I am assuming the paraphernalia in the bathroom is not yours....or your mother's' I mumbled with embarrassment on my return to the lounge.

'Oh ya drongo teesha, it's me ball an' chain's'.

'And she is WHERE precisely?' I enquired.

'SHOPPING'

'But not in town surely' I nervously stammered.

'Yeah' was the inconvenient reply

'Did she say when she would be back' I asked with mounting panic.

'Oh sheeel be ages, she's a reel dag for shoppin'.…. prob'ly late arvo at least' he drawled.

It was 12.30 and all thoughts of having a spiffing time and getting paid for it faded and in its place a major tension migraine arrived.

There is not a section in the Hooker's handbook which says: 'How to handle a potential disaster without having a contretemps with the tosser who created it'.

Funny how one can go from wet vagina to angina.

The stress was KILLING me.

'Toss- Testicles' was BLOODY GETTING OFF ON IT!!!!! The thought of BEING CAUGHT was making his pre cum seep through his moleskins.

I'm not supposed to nag my customers, but his jolly jape was endangering my health.

'Look, I can't relax...I'm waiting for the key in the door...I won't be able to come (he had indicated my pleasure was HIS pleasure)'.

He made soothing noises and started to seduce me....and you know what...after a sustained and prolonged fabulous spot of frottage, my legs were akimbo and inviting the first of several earth shattering orgasms for the afternoon.

I felt so good I frankly DID NOT GIVE A GIRAFFE'S GENITALS for what would happen if his shopping Sheila arrived back before I had earned not only a shit load of dollars but broken the record for girlie ghee expelled in a 4 hour period.

Yes, sometimes things in life go horribly wrong and sometimes a fraught situation exceeds all expectations. It was hard however, to see where my current life experience would leave me.

'When 'ave you gotta see the Sapphic Sisters again?' my mate Harry of 'Turbo Sperm fame' indecorously enquired.

'Just because they are all stay press trousers and white shirts----doesn't mean they are Lesbians Harry' I replied.

'Who else would do that bleedin' job' he retorted

I GUESS HE HAD A POINT.

RIM WITH A VIEW

'I believe you have something with my name on it?' I asked in my most imperious and mock tones.

Matching mock tones were volleyed back: 'If your name is Moet Rose, then by all means we can accommodate you my good lady'.

This was my local Convenience Store, and by golly it was indeed handy they were so close, since I could not catch my breath with the bogeyman of anxiety clogging my windpipe.

It was only 11am, but the only remedy seemed a glass of bubbles. If I had to self-combust in a nervous breakdown ----I was going to crumple in style.

That stance may have been borne of an upbringing where, faced with only one pair of shoes, one makes liberal use of Meltonian White or Kiwi Polish to put a shine on a poor ass turd.

I was due for another going over at the hands of the appointed Governmental Goons, and was waiting for my 'Whore Whisperer' to utter words of encouragement before my second session commenced.

It was a most clement day. Indeed, the kind of morning when you recognise the reason why the rent, which is equal to the national debt of any potentate, is worth the burden.

A cloudless day with a perfect optimum temperature of 25C degrees, and a zero wind factor (my sphincter muscle exempted) was the pre-setting for this second gladiatorial locking of horns.

There was an eerie stillness and calm before the storm. The horizon was hazily melting into the sea---and I felt myself melting with it. It was amazing what a pre lunchtime gulp of Champagne could do.

I idly glanced to my right and saw in the distance my legal beagle. He was many hundreds of yards away, but he employed the exact gait of the 'out of towner'.

This is a walk I have witnessed many times. The steps scream the words: 'Oh, golly, look at the sea, it's so good to get away from the hell hole of the city, I could just roll my trousers up and have a little paddle. I really fancy falling asleep in a deck chair after having consumed a Mr Whippy. I really should get away more often'.

These words and more were encapsulated in the sauntering stride of my Solicitor. He looked like a child bursting to get into either his swimming trunks or on a white knuckle ride at the funfair. It was the walk of wonderment, whereas we cynics took for granted the sense of wide open spaces and the sea air.

Somehow it felt silly to break the spell with talk of criminal proceedings and fiscal fandangos. We sat on my balcony in mutual silence punctuated with pleasantries, chit chat and, as usual, the odd wave to passers-by.

I saw a few of the street drinkers congregating in the bus shelter on the opposite side of the road and remembered a day, much like this one, when I had a very funny experience........

The number of men that I had inveigled to join me in my 'lair', purely from sitting on my balcony, was ....ONE.

Having imbibed a few refreshing G&T's from mid-afternoon to sunset, I was relaxed and all was well in the universe.

From across the road I espied a likely lad, who saw me luxuriating at my opulent and splendiferous vantage point--and crossed the road, intent upon making my acquaintance.

He looked like a cheeky scallywag, with a cheery smile and oversized unlaced bovver boots.......

'Gee, I'd love to join you in a drink up there' he shouted.

I looked down, and couldn't help but smile at the *NERVE* of the guy.

'Don't move' I cried.

Thirty seconds later (as he stood expectantly at the door of the building) I threw down to him a *BIC RAZOR.*

'Get your self shaved' I demanded.

'No way, he remonstrated, 'I've had my beard and moustache for ever'.

'Then you'll be on your way I expect' I called, as I closed my French window balcony doors in faux petulance.

After 5, 10 or maybe 15 minutes, (I guess while he wrestled with his manhood, conscience and proposed sex life), I watched him slope off into the distance.

Thirty minutes later, he was back, with a spring in his step, which said: 'I've just fought the crusades and now I have come to have my way with YOU, woman'.

My throat tightened--this was SSSOOOOOOOOoooo exciting!!!!!

I let him in. I have never seen a more pathetic figure in my entire life.

He may have sacrificed his hirsute manhood for me, but he had also cut his face to within 3 strokes of anaemia through severe blood loss.

'All the toilets were closed, I had to do it with cold water' he wailed.

And a right mess he had made too.

I made like Flo nightingale, and by the time I had tidied up the topiary of his face I was overcome by: fatigue, sun and playing 'MUM' to a prospective lover.

'If you want to stay, then that's fine, but lay one hand on me and you are a dead man!!---Is that clear???' I barked.

For once, I found a man who did what he was told.

In the morning (he had an early job interview) he slowly aroused me and---ahem---was a very UNSELFISH LOVER.

Now let's get this euphemism straight---he gave me beautiful, soft, gentle, wet,- caring-- (and any other adjective you can think of) oral------and did not require the same in return.

Four hours later, he was back. He had left a one quarter full, bottle of cider in my fridge---and had *COME TO PICK IT UP.*

I was too happy and tired to wonder why----but all became apparent 8 hours later.

It was a tradition (until I bloody well changed it) for a church association to feed the waifs, strays and homeless--adjacent to my apartment.

My eyes fixed upon an UNLACED PAIR OF BOVVER BOOTS, in the scrum of the dispossessed feeding frenzy.

Some weeks later, an acerbic mate of mine opined: 'must hand it to ya, you are an equal opportunity kind of gal.'

Yep, I had taken in the 'homeless' for one night.

I WOULD NEVER LIVE IT DOWN!!

Back to the present, I had one last swig of Dutch courage and bade farewell to the glorious vista. I had a date with destiny and psyched myself up for another portion of humble pie.

ONE LEGGED ARSE KICKER

'You did really well, you controlled the interview'.

This was the view of my brief.

It was a suspiciously short interlude with Frick and Frack on our second 'grilling', and as me and Whore Whisperer strolled down the road with for a well-earned libation, there was a temporary feeling of relief that I had endured jump 2 of an entire (potential) Grand National.

We asked more questions about each other's lives and the subject of 'Bed Sheet' inevitably reared its hydra like head.

'How did you meet him?' There it was again. What were the steps that led me to seek his accountancy skills?

I slyly grinned. This was a leading question which was asked by rote, and by so many people, that I wondered at the significance of how you actually chose a person who puts the books in order.

'It was an existing customer' I said. Realising it sounded like I was describing one of my patrons, I added: 'Of HIS'

He gave a nod and a knowing smile, so to spice the information I threw the dog a bone.

'He's (the customer) actually just in the middle of a rather messy divorce' I put my palm dramatically on my chest adding 'though it's absolutely nothing to do with me'.

This elicited another grin. If only he could have been there..........

Oh, the Oirish cock of my 'accountant finder' was the Cristal of champers and the Kobe beef of steak with a backstage pass to THE BEATLES, DEEP PURPLE AND THE WHO rolled into one

What a beautiful dick!!!

A thing of beauty is a joy forever they say...it was mine for at least this afternoon.

It bore no resemblance to Quasimodo, a button mushroom, or a frill-necked lizard.

It was just perfectly PRETTY.

However, I still had to reconcile the majesty of the beast to the idiot that was unfortunately attached to it.

I normally boycotted blokes from his geographical neck of the woods. Experience had taught me that the misery of the experience was not worth the money gained.

What made me think it would be any different in an environment outside of fiscal frivolity?

It was a gross error in judgment.

There are numerous sex guides to help with etiquette on the 'work bench'.

He either was illiterate, naive or didn't give a toss.

He was like an unruly child who has forgotten the Ritalin for his Attention Deficit Disorder...he simply WOULD NOT BEHAVE. HE WAS THE KIND OF PERSON WHO WOULD HAVE TEA AT BUCKINGHAM PALACE AND WOULD THEN THROW CREAM CAKES AT THE QUEEN AND KICK HER CORGIS IN THE GONADS.

My attempts to adore it (the wonderful willy) orally were constantly interrupted and any 'riding of the wild tiger' was tempered by constantly being on the lookout for him ripping 'the protection' off.

Had this been a Formula One race, the safety car would be out, the yellow flags would be frantically waving and he would have been ordered to Pit...and in the 8 seconds it takes for a tyre change, they could have dragged the rookie driver from the cockpit and replaced him with a crash test dummy

We somehow reached a 1-1 orgasmic scoreline...and miraculously I shelved my irritation long enough to be (much later) 2-1 up when in exhaustion and a kind of sick ecstasy, my head lolled to the side...and I noticed the time.

Fuck!!!!!

I was on air...... the BBC was waiting for my *Vox Copuli* on proposed sex laws ....I ran to the living room....the 'opposing team' followed, thinking he was Man. United, and attempted to come from behind and draw in the dying embers of play.

'Bugger off' I snarled

With the phone clamped to one ear while the other ear heard my nemesis searching for the detritus of his hastily discarded attire, BBC Southern Counties informed me I would be required imminently and a fantasy which was 7 months in the making stumbled out of the door without so much as a kiss my arse goodbye.........

I've heard of star crossed lovers. We must have been logic starved hedonists.

A match made in heaven for sure.

What perverse prats would repeat that performance?

Us two, that's who.

We met again within days.

What kind of madness would make us do it TWICE!!!!!!!!

But we did, 'to be sure to be sure' as my Oirish 'da' would say.

By the end I felt like a cross between a HSBC night deposit facility and a used, damp, screwed up snot rag.

His departure bore the indecency of haste which is the guilty badge of the married man.

It was an 'EMPTY' and I was the receptacle....well not QUITE the receptacle...there is some quaint Modus Operandi whereby on the vinegar stroke, and in one swift movement, the twat relieves his testicles ALL OVER WHAT EVER PIECE OF FLESH HE CAN FIND ON THE OTHER PARTICIPANT.

It has to be something learnt at the mother's knee (or breast)....'THOUGH SHALT NOT SULLY ONE'S OWN BODY WITH THINE OWN BABY BATTER'.

The upside being, I cancelled my chemical peel and exfoliation session. My fair skin suffered the abrasions of hubba -hubba -hubba 'let's swop spit and weld our very souls with a prolonged snogerama'.

L'oreal and Revlon would do well to head hunt this gobshite!!!

The score line ended at 4-3 in my favour (hurrah)...though he says his last goal didn't count since I 'gave no input' (try telling my jaw that) and that he had to practically dribble the ball from one end of the pitch to the other without so much as a kick or a header from me'

Everything happens for a reason, and though I would rather stick molten coals up my butt than repeat the encounters, he was the person who came to my assistance when I needed help.

Boy, did I earn it! But did I DESERVE what was happening in my Bad Karma life?

PUSH ME, PULL YOU

I once met a man who had taking a proven 'quit smoking' campaign to various countries around the world. The key to its success was a definite number. Naturally it was so long ago I cannot recall the precise figure (maybe it was 15), but it was in fact the number of days it took the brain to re- programme itself to not even THINK of a nicotine fix ever again.

Sensing a marketing opportunity in the making, I feel the time has come to take my: DAYS BEFORE A NERVOUS BREAKDOWN WILL ENSUE WHEN UNDER A TAX INVESTIGATION AND CRIMINAL PROSECUTION on the road........

I reckon the figure is approximately 169.

The revenue KNOW it is, because they are sure to have a 'Q' James Bond like 'jobs worth' figure, deep in the bowls of the Special Investigations Unit who has adjudged this equation for the benefit of the Government.

This is the time to apply the pressure, when the snivelling wretch is it its weakest.

It is the reason why the 'Bill' employ the tactic of 'Dawn Raids' and why many techniques used in the extraction of information rely on the poor sap being at its lowest ebb.

And this, with me, was indeed the case.

I could easily have confessed to knowing the whereabouts of Lord Lucan or even Shergar, except....except........

'APPLE DOES NOT FALL FAR FROM TREE' Confucius he says........

My middle name is 'perversity'....named after my Father.......who would have responded in the same way.

I was frankly tired of being made to Kowtow through fear, and hated the balance of power being so one sided, when I had not (bar a few grand) done anything wrong.

Now they were just making me plain ANGRY.

I made a trip to the Post Office, skidding as usual on the Dog detritus, and queuing as usual with smelly people who never washed their clothes, let alone their bodies.

I was afforded a piece of luck, and was accompanied by a lady acquaintance who told me she was the very next day: 'going to Paris for lunch'.

'Oh, what a coincidence, I'm going to Edinburgh for Lunch' I exclaimed. We congratulated ourselves on being mighty decadent, and I discovered that her trip was going to be with about 30 OTHER ladies 'of a certain age', from THE RED HAT SOCIETY.

This 'club' was formed originally in America and it takes its name from a well-known poem:

> When I am an old woman I shall wear purple with a red hat
> which doesn't go, and doesn't suit me.
> And I shall spend my pension
> on brandy and summer gloves and satin sandals,
> And say we've no money for butter.
> I shall sit down on the pavement when I'm tired
> and gobble up samples in shops
> and press alarm bells
> and run with my stick along public railings,
> and make up for the sobriety of my youth.
>
> I shall go out in my slippers in the rain
> and pick flowers in other people's gardens......

You get the picture.

The manifesto blurb reads that:

"The Red Hat Society began as a result of a few women deciding to greet middle age with verve, humour and élan. We believe silliness is the comedy relief of life, and since we are all in it together, we might as well join red-gloved hands and go for the gusto together. Underneath the frivolity, we share a bond of affection, forged by common life experiences and a genuine enthusiasm for wherever life takes us next." ....that was the just the ticket for me!!!!

In my haste I dashed off a quick jaunty/frivolous email to the chapter 'Mother' of Brighton Belle' enthusing:

> *'That poem has always been one of my favourites.*
> *Question: Do you accept Erotic service providers???*
> *My current profession has never been an issue with people (I even interviewed the Mayor and Mayoress some months back)......*
> *But I thought I ought to ask.*
> *I have also been put down to 'perform' for the festival of age (though not in that sense) with Dora Bryan....I have a red hat and purple clothing...so I'm a shoo in really. Please let me know your decision.*
> *Letitcia*

www.maturebustyblonde.co.uk (even my website is red and purple)'

Well I waited and waited and waited for a reply............in fact I waited so long, I had used all my Gillette G2 blades along with most of my Wilkinson Intuition and Venus ones too!!!

In truth I knew I had been ignored, and when I rang to enquire what was happening, I instantly knew from the terse and guarded reception that I was persona non grata

Of course she lied (how I HATE that) and I sweetly offered to send it AGAIN.

This is an abridged version of her reply:

> 'I don't have an issue with what you do. I think it should be legalised (maybe it is now I don't know) as there is a big market for your kind of service.
> I am afraid I would not visit your web site as I don't want anything of a sexual nature on my computer and I wouldn't want to be bombarded with web sites of a sexual nature. I would not want the Brighton Belles or the Red Hat Society colours of red & purple to be associated with anything like that.
> It's bad enough now when some people say "Red Hat no Drawers" and in fact one listener rang BBC Southern Counties Radio and said that exotic service providers during the second world war wore red hats as during the black out, they would be more easily recognised, and that's where the saying comes from.
> When we meet as a group what we do or did as an occupation comes up in conversation and I do not feel it would be appropriate for the Brighton Belles. So I have to say no to joining us at this time'
> Regards---------

Jesus!! I had been thrown out of better shit holes than THAT....I was not best pleased...I emailed back:

> 'It was good of you to take the time and trouble to respond.
> What I do is totally legal.
> It is not the only thing that I do.
> I have written articles for many national and local newspapers and magazines and also I do stand-up comedy and after dinner speaking.
> I have an issue with misguided and ignorant prejudice, and accordingly I will take this up with the European Community (I am au fait with law), as your response has shown that my basic Human rights are being violated'
> L

OOOh, that put her papal purple in a dizzying spin. Handbags at dawn!!!!!

She parried with a flustered 'don't threaten me' email, but then (presumably having made fraught calls (to other members) made another perfunctory stab at civility.

'Let's start again. It's not because of your threats but I realise I may have been rather hasty and some of my comments may have been hurtful to you.
That is not the kind of person I am, and I do not hold grudges either, hence: my invitation to you to forget the past and start anew.
You could give me your phone number so we could have a chat face to face.
Otherwise, tell me a little bit more about you.
Your age, interests, hobbies, any children or grandchildren etc. This is what I ask all new ladies who show an interest to join.
I look forward to hearing from you'.

I decided to reply with the greatest of courtesy, and concluded in reply with the words:

'It's not a biggie, I accept your decision (begrudgingly).....or maybe you can throw it open to the members to decide????'

NOW THAT WAS SEVERAL MONTHS AGO!!!!!
I have now made a decision of my own.
To paraphrase Groucho Marx: I do not wish to belong to a club that would accept me as a member.
I mean, COME ON!!!!
I'm not asking for centre court tickets at the Wimbledon finals....nor backstage passes for The Monsters of Rock or Ozzfest.
I have decided to start my own.
THE GREY PUBE CLUB, or THE RED TWAT SOCIETY will not be run by, or have a membership of judgemental bints.
We will bear that particular moniker due to tireless pursuit of sexual pleasure.
Our twats will be red due to: WANKING, SHAGGING, LICKING, SPANKING-----and a cornucopia of nefarious sexual activities.
Our lovers must be at least half, or (ideally) a third of our age.
This is where our experience counts.
We will seduce and educate the over 16 yr olds, who....lets face it...are sick to their blue bollocks of a perfunctory lick on the tip of their bell end.
Golden oldies know the drill, and we can administer the most replete deep throat this side of the black stump.
I related this tale of overt bigotry to an American mate of mine, saying that the club originated in the USA.
He said: 'Red NECK Society', more like........
It was hard to know where I fitted in. According to HMRC, I was subject to the laws of sole trading the same as any other tax payer. But, I was treated as a second class (make that no class AT ALL) citizen.

I discovered that I was deemed persona non grata by nearly everybody (along with existing patrons) after I had completed my book: BODY WORSHIP.

I didn't know my place

Memories of that time were written about in affectionate terms, and one or two characters were even lauded as 'never to be forgotten'

I especially wanted to track down Mr Yashimoto……..

FOUR SHALLOW, FIFTH DEEP

He was the man for whom I had held a candle for many years. The first cut may indeed be the deepest, but the first man to cut it in the lovemaking department deserves a congressional medal of honour.

My mates Google and Yahoo at the World Wide Web came to the rescue, and I tracked the hapless Nippon down.

He had given a talk as guest speaker at the Melbourne Hilton several years previous, and although his Japanese name was the British equivalent of 'John smith' ....I did not think it could belong to another. He had done well for himself.

He was practically Minister of Tourism. Well, he could make a second world tour of my hinterland, incorporating added side trips, with impunity.

'Never go back' they say. There seemed nothing to look forward to, so I 'drank and dialled'.

I inevitably got his Japanese Personal Secretary. I showed her that even a worthless 'Gaijin' could talk a smattering of 'Nihon-jin'

'Moshi moshi, watachi no nama e wa Letitcia-San desu'. The 5 seconds time delay which is the curse of international phone calls----stretched to 10.

This was because most Japanese people cannot believe that anyone is on their language radar. There is an innate 'we are better than the rest of the world, even though we are shorter, and our men have dicks the size of a tape worm, and our women have legs the shape of a radish, and we committed the most outrageous war crimes......we are descendents of the Emperor....and are therefore superior' mentality.

So, to speak in their language is a curiosity to them.

'Herro Retitcia-San, where you rearn to spik our ranguage?' Ms Secretary asked.

'Watachi no Koibito' was the answer, though the 'koibito' (lover) in question----was her boss.

She put me through, --------this was it....after all these years, a reunion with the 'dogs bollocks of doin' it right on the futon work bench'.

'Herro?' a worried voice said.

'Yashimoto'...it's ME.....Letitcia-San!!'

The 5 and 10 second delay stretched to about twenty. An even MORE worried voice asked: 'How you get number???'

This, quite frankly, was not the response I wanted from the distant man of my dreams.

I blathered on about my life advancements, book, etc.....I wanted to show him that just because he could buy me by the hour for a fee in Australia, I had tried at least to moved on......

'I even mentioned you in my Book, I said you was the best lover in world' were the words I used to try to get an inside track on the man who was not (despite our sexual history) warming to my impromptu call.

'I hope book does not come to Japan or Austraria' he commented

With these words, and the vague insinuation that the purpose of the call was that of a blackmailing nature, he comprehensively trampled on the last vestiges of imagined romance. He morphed from a kind and impossibly affectionate lover to a cruelty and dispassion befitting that of a shrill prisoner of war commandant.

He repeatedly barked the mantra: 'YOU HAVE TO PLOTECT MY FAMIRLY'

Bloody hell, I didn't know THAT was in the massage parlour guidelines. I had imagined that every man visiting and paying a sex worker had squared away in his brain the 'quid pro quo'. Yashimoto's 'quid' was rapidly downward spiralling to a fifty pence piece.

He was wide open to the comment: 'Well, you actually DID have a family who you used to abandon with much regularity way back then------I guess our memories are not as selective' (though I had far too much class to go for his Japanese jugular), so when he asked that I wait until he emailed me on a PRIVATE emailing system, I knew what I had to do.

I saw his snappy bark and raised it to a growl which emanated from my solar plexus.

'THAT WON'T BE NECESSARY BECAUSE WE WILL NEVER SPEAK TO EACH OTHER AGAIN'. And what was worse was......I meant it.

Ten minutes later, 'Bed Sheet' rang to tell me how his meeting with the 'Complex Business Crime Unit' had fared. I guess I should have felt honoured that someone with such an 'impressive' title had deemed it a priority to travel all the way to Brighton to look into my fiscal affairs.

Basically CBCU ripped to shreds all accounts, expenditure and income estimations that had taken me months to compile and came in with a figure at 5 times the amount.

'Gotta go, I have a Golden shower due in 5 minutes------and I've peaked early' were the words that bought to a close one of the most important phone calls of my life.

A romantic dream was lost while a litigation nightmare was brewing and the ever present was pressing on my bladder.

My world was shit.

GASH AND GARY

'Desire is the only thing that keeps you young' beamed my irrepressible doctor as I struggled with the menopause several years previously. I made a mental note to insert a dipstick digit in my front botty each day-----just to check I was still half alive.

He was a walking- talking advert for good health, positive thoughts and Karmic thinking.

Yoga, stress management and Ayevedic/Eastern Homeopathic medicine was his passion.

Yes, no matter what ailed the patient (I had co patient friends who experienced the same), herb tinctures or exotic powders from India were somehow pressed home in one's vulnerable moments.

This time I wasn't buying, in fact, I broke down in tears.

I needed help. I had not masturbated in aeons, and I imagined my clitoris was taking a well earned nap of a life time, complete with bobble hat and scarf, securely tucked away from my dreaded right hand.

The thought of sucking dick appalled me and I wanted the world and the Tax man to leave me the fuck alone.

As a sex worker, this was a slight problem and the mother of all drawbacks.

Clinical depression had finally bitten me on my ample arse.

'What would you do in my situation Doctor' I sniffled

'I have my faith-----and I trust in the universe, whatever will be------ will be' he told me with a beaming smile.

'But I'm tired of being afraid all the time, and I fear the outcome. I feel helpless and hopeless' I whispered, reaching for more tissues.

'I think you need some extra help' said Dr Snake Oil

I knew what he meant, he wanted me to be a fully laid up member of the pill popping classes. At least when the ignorant proletariat viewed prostitutes as druggies, I took solace in the fact that I did not fit neatly into that pathetic preconception.

Now, with me, they would for once be semi correct.

This made me sob some more, but the prescription was written with the words: 'I've had some great results with this' and he very kindly GAVE me one of his mystical concoctions to spray on my face whenever I felt a panic attack rising.

'I need a petrol tanker full of this' I thought.

A week later I bumped into an ex neighbour who, for very different reasons, was ALSO on Anti-depressants.

We had a hollow guffaw at the fact that I was walking one way up the street, he the other------but we were BOTH trying not to cry.

We were a duo of quivering chins and wept tears of hilarity and gloom in equal measure. To make matters worse, we were in one of the most miserable bus shelters (that takes nature's rejects and asbo adolescents back to their burned out car and crime infested council estate) that Brighton can offer.

The baby breeders glowered at us and the spotty oiks made unwanted 'fucking nutters' like comments.

He described how one feels before medication 'kicks into the system'

'Which ones did they give you......do you feel any better' he asked.

'I don't know the name of them, to tell you the truth, and anyway, I haven't taken my prescription to the chemist yet' I admitted.

'Why not'?

'I'm too depressed' I replied with a glib smile.

Five minutes later I found myself in familiar territory: ON MY HANDS AND KNEES WITH A NINE INCH PHALLUS IN MY HAND.

The difference being, it was bright yellow and had the word 'Fair Trade' plastered all over it. Yep, it was a banana.

I had fallen foul of a grape in aisle 7 of Somerfield Supermarket, and gone arse over tit.

The British faller follows the same Modus operandi------getting up quickly before anyone thinks they look like a prat.

Too late!!

My hat skidded like a Frisbee, and my arse was inviting any likely lad to fill its opening.

I looked around for someone, anyone, to assist a woman with a worryingly damaged knee.

There were no takers, this is England, and no kind soul wanted to get involved

'Let's get ready to rumble' was the message which sprung to life over the internal tannoy system.

Now, this message (I had, through years of supermarket shopping, worked out the less than secret code) is usually reserved for pilferers.

The security announcement was now being used to help a floozie in the process of fingering their food.

A rather disinterested young man with a face that screamed: 'Less on chocolate and more on acne remedies' stood and watched me as I slowly regained what was left of my composure.

'I want to fill out an incident form' I said.

I may just as well have said: 'I want to take an umbrella and ram it down the eye of your dick. Then want to OPEN it.'

He didn't look very happy.

After he begrudgingly took my statement I hobbled out the door.

I knew one person in the whole of Brighton who could make me laugh, and as luck would have it, he was within hobbling distance.

I would have to withstand a constant disco beat and the effluent of a hardened chain smoker, but he was worth it.

WOULD YOU LIKE SOME ONION WITH THAT MINCE?

If Billy Connolly ever mated with Lily Savage, Tone (nicknamed 'Vitriol and Violets') would be their two headed love child.

Manager of a 'Gay lifestyle' outlet, he could scythe the universe with a pithy aside, with no discernable effort.

He surveyed my limp and said: 'Rough night last night love?'

This awakened my chuckle muscle and once he knew he had me on the ropes he piled on the foul mouthed momentum.

'Did you not think of retiring love' he continued 'one phone call from me to Age Concern and you'll be sitting in yer 'pishy knickers in a home for elderly prossies'.

I knew he loved me really, and that he reserved his most vile diatribes for those whom he had a sneaking regard.

He showed his Glaswegian compassion when I had shown him the Original wrongly addressed letter (MRS indeed) from the Ministry of Migraine.

'I don't know why you're looking so worried love' he leered 'I'll be in court for support, when they snatch that hat of yours off your Tax Avoiding head, and drag you down to cells. I bet some hair extensions come out an' all'.

Oh he thought it was beyond hilarious.

'What's with the cripple look?' he sneered.

I mentioned my fall in the supermarket and the sneer turned to distaste. 'You don't shop THERE love, surely to God, business can't be THAT bad----I would have thought Waitrose at the very least'.

He minced around the counter to shuffle some R18 Porn Video's and a familiar face came in view.

Oh yes, I remembered hiring a male escort and getting this particular shirt lifter with an impossibly huge scaling and an even bigger ego. There he was, on a video cover, on a calendar, and a book.

'I've had him' I noted 'and it was the worst punt of my life'.

The staff all looked at one another, then at me. Tone was just about to slay me with another bitchy barb when he stopped mid thought and exclaimed: 'Did you WALK here?'

I was confused.

'Well, as best I could, what with my knee an' all' I replied.

'Do I teach you silly bitches NOTHING, you're meant to stay down until an ambulance comes, you'll see no compo if that knee of yours doesn't mend'.

I told him it was the least of my worries, and after a few more jokes delivered at my expense, I hobbled home.

The next day the sum of all fears came true. My knee was buggered, and since I had a prior appointment with a gentleman who adored slow and sensual sucking of his genitalia, I was in abject misery.

At first, when the might of the Taxation Tyrants pressed down on my unsuspecting apology for a life, the only discernable fallout was of the psychological variety. I didn't want to work anymore. Now, I COULDN'T-----I was in too much pain.

Of course I tried to disguise it: the high heeled stilettos were discarded once my paying customers' back were turned, I asked for assistance in getting up from the couch…citing a non existent cramp. In short, it was like inviting Granny to bed.

The champion of vile verbiage (Tone) was his normal helpful self.

'I'm not going to kid you love, but you need to get back to basics and 'holler for a dollar'.

'How do you mean' I asked.

'You're SUPPOSEDLY a sex worker, right?'

'I Guess' I replied guardedly.

'THEN WOULD IT PAIN YOU TOO MUCH TO SUPPLY SOME OF IT THEN SWEET CHEEKS?'

'I don't do anything of an invasive or penetrative nature' I parried.

He flounced round the counter and started unpacking rubber G Strings and 'Poppers' disguised as room deodorisers, turned as an afterthought and growled: 'Then you should think of trying another profession'.

Taking stock of my situation: My mind was irreparably damaged and my Body was running out of orifices to invade---and moreover, positions in which to provide them.

Finally, my bank balance was waning each rental month.

This was what was fashionably called: 'behind the eight ball', and it sucked.

The supermarket eventually offered me a derisory sum to quell my distress (£50) and since I was several grand out of pocket, I begrudgingly asked the Whore Whisperer if he knew of a personal injury dude in his firm.

He not only delivered, but, yet again, I had a wonderful member of team Letitcia to help stave off the sling and arrows of outrageous misfortune.

'Band Aid' (as I named him) made my acquaintance and we set my SECOND litigation lorry rolling.

The bills were piling up and I had to make yet another visit to various banks, to not only pay the darned things, but to extract the money to do so.

How my life had changed!

Banks used to be such an exciting place to be, and I had written a blog about it several months previous, entitled……… : 'Sexy Secretary meets Bonking Bank Chief:

As follows:

IT WAS A CRAZY THING TO DO..........So I was the woman for the job..........

I will never understand the willingness powerful men (or those in positions of high regard) have for living dangerously.

They are almost megalomaniacal in their quest for sailing as close to a sodding hurricane as they possibly can.

'Come to my office dressed as a secretary' the bank manager enthused

I love a bit of fun, so dressed in a severe black suit with cream lace 'body' (the ones with poppers at the crotch), matching gloves (even in 44%C heat) pearls, hair piled in a severe beehive, stockings (oh yes) lizard skin (classy bird that I am) court shoes and studious glasses...I announced myself to HIS secretary.

I carried a brief case but all manner of sexual paraphernalia was inside.

Yes, we did the 'crawl under the desk and blow me while asking a colleague about something important' fantasy.

Yes we did the 'turn the desk around so I can munch your shaven haven while looking at the view of the Harbour Skyline' thang

Yes we did the 'bang me from behind in front of the two way mirror which overlooked his workers' scene.

Yes we did the 'take a letter and a spanking Ms Jones because your last correspondence had errors' schtick.

You name it we luxuriated and gorged on the feast that was NAUGHTINESS.

I didn't count on the finale, that which finds us riding the elevator (no pun) of the tall glass and chrome monument...with me reaching behind and pleasuring his (I thought) depleted AND spent cock with my lace gloves.

Each time the lift stopped, he somehow gained a perceptible measure of turgidity when another person entered the confined elevator domain.

We reached the bottom (ground floor)...but he wanted to go back to the top, so excited was he by the intrusion of different people temporarily entering our space.

This was all well and good....until one of his opposite numbers came (I mean 'got in') in the lift and motioned that he had to see him urgently.

No problem you would think.

WRONG.

My Southern Belle lacy gloves had decided to weld themselves to his zip.

Why do I always find myself in the middle of a sexual farce of 'Carry On', 'Benny Hill', 'Are you being served' and ''allo 'allo' proportions?????

I gave a few frantic tugs but couldn't release the exquisite French lace.

His opposite number indicated that he wanted him to join him on urgent business immediately, so, since I was supposed to be a mere stranger travelling with Mr Bank of the Southern Hemisphere, I had to sacrifice my classy hand wear.

With one swift jerk (it had to be the ultimate jerk off)....I exited the corporate building looking like a Michael Jackson reject.

I had sacrificed my fashion sense for a Master of the Universe with a jagged zip.

One week later he reunited me with the said glove.

It was ripped and covered in spunk.

Glory days of pleasure and wilful hedonism had now been replaced by paranoia and potentially suicidal tendencies.

Ah yes,' the days of wine and roses are not long'.

But, bloody Christmas comes around every year.......

MUM'S THE WORD

How I dread the festive season which is supposedly the celebration of Baby Jesus's birth. I geographically avoided it while in Australia, but there was still the 'Giri' (Japanese social obligation) of the dreaded international phone call home, and the sobs of my Mother burning up the worldwide airwaves.

I would try to diffuse the tears with:

'Can you cry a bit faster Mother, this call is costing a fortune', but this would open the sluice gates for another twenty dollars of sniffling.

One way or another, there was just no escaping the lachrymose element at the family home of Letitcia.

Comfort and joy my arse.

Mother had the peculiar habit of tearing round the small kitchen with a grim look of determination, and the merest hint of Martyrdom, to complete the arduous task of washing up------- BEFORE the main event of the day.

'THE QUEEN'S SPEECH'.

How we ribbed the bejeezus out of her.

We were unspeakably cruel. We would either: lock her out of the TV room, or act the goat, unplug the bugger, and inform her that it had broken down.

We thought it was a jolly jape and had a great laugh at her expense.

It is funny how life changes.

Now, years later, when we enquire as to if she is ready to watch her Majesty, she will snort from the kitchen 'What do I want to look at HER for?'

We cajole her even further by pointing out that the ridiculous 'Royal Watcher' from the village (who had been on a 30 odd year vigil to watch the Royal party walk to church (and back) at Sandringham) might be on telly.

'She I'n't roite in the head' would be Mum's Norfolk accented refrain.

Christmas 2006 was shaping up to beyond unbearable. I was out of forced bonhomie, or sense of celebration and there seemed to be nothing to look forward to.

Prior to the annual pilgrimage to Norfolk, my mate Julie B invited me for lunch. She made the most extraordinarily kind gesture/offer of money to me.

'This isn't ABOUT money' I growled 'it is a slow, systematic, sadistic road to hell for the person they target. I just happen to be that person. Keep your money'.

She leaned closer, looked from left to right and all points North and South in the restaurant and asked knowingly: 'You comin' back to my place?'

This was a euphemism for: 'Do you want to get so fucked up that you will be crawling home in 72 hours' time'

Now, in this life, there are few things that can pay the last two inflated instalments of council tax and provide enough pleasure to provide a temporary smile for my dial.

I therefore declined the thoughtful offer. I had a date with 'sexual healing' at it's finest.

The only generic thing, (bar copious amounts of Class 'A's and ten flagons of vintage Champagne) that could soothe the savage beast of a soul in abject agony, was a date with Jason.

Actually, it wasn't so much a date as an appointment.

He was 18 yrs old and a cute as a pair of lace panties.

I was playing busty school mistress to lusty schoolboy, so it was out with the fully-fashioned silk seamed stockings, white blouse and black pencil skirt.

He even liked the 'School Ma'm' spectacles pushed down on my nose as I licked his testicles and all points north. I idly wondered if this had happened for real. He was a very cute boy, with a butt that screamed: 'munch me for half an hour'......and I was all ears.

But first, I had to torture him with the '500 lines for Miss' fantasy and 'I MUST NOT PEEK AT TEACHER'S TITS' was the sentence he had to write over and over again.

He started off well enough. His writing was neat and horizontal, but within a few teasing undone buttons of my teacher blouse, his lines were going diagonally, while his dick was vertical.

When I checked my seams were straight, his exercise book was catapulted by 11 inches (he was a huge boy) of throbbing lust and skidded clear across the 'schoolroom' floor

'That will be another 200 lines' I purred.

OOOhhh, the tension was electric, though the problem being, I was so 'hot to trot' that I abandoned the extra lines after 25 pathetic scrawls......

He was a Virgin 3 times removed (by me), yet he had the soft tender touch of....a guaranteed orgasm.

There was something glorious about so much pleasure and excitement coming from an almost chaste experience. I'm not sure if his Mum had told him that all women had teeth in their vaginas (a common ploy used by Mothers to keep their Sons' sexually innocent), but he didn't want any penetration.

He simply revelled in caressing my body and 'sucking face' and in fact, he could nearly make me come by the act of kissing alone.

When this extended foreplay was combined with the mantra : 'You are so beautiful' from such a sweet looking lad, I was very wet putty (and pussy) in his hands.

I refrained from asking the 'would you care to lick a little further south' leading question, that is, until I thought I would implode with Head Teacher desire.

'Have you ever gone down on a woman?' I asked

His reply was all I had hoped for: 'No, but I'd love to go down on you' He smiled at he thought that he could show off his technique, and seemed proud the teacher was treating him like a 'grown up'

All I can say is, he must have practised for hours with the yielding flesh of a pomegranate, or the viscous consistency of sliced fig. This boy rocked. If this was his first foray at the furburger, then the rest of mankind should bow its head in reverence---and women kind should look out.

What a Kid!!!

I walked around in a fluffy, 'Jason induced' stupor for days after, until I could not put off entering the gates of 'Happy Christmas Hell'

Staying away would have monumentally cruel, and the guilt alone would have been worse than actually going through the Merry Xmas motion.

For five days, I was a dutiful daughter and kept my anxiety and anguish (for the most part) inside.

Mind you, it was in some ways an improvement of the previous year............

Most families would have a mantel piece full of heartfelt salutations from loved ones.

Not the Letitcia family. Ours was full of 'advice sheets' from the local Accident and Emergency department of The Queen Elizabeth Hospital.

Did we have a death wish or were we accident PRONE??

Not really.

Christmas eve morning found the rude awakening of my mother shouting in a quavering, tremulous voice for me to come downstairs 'quickly'.

'What the fuck now' I thought.

The Norfolk constabulary had thoughtfully saved my brother from either danger to his wellbeing or at the very least an expensive taxi fare home.

(If you feel the latter is a handy ruse, then simply walk (stagger) in the middle of a main road and they will deliver you to your door.)

Unfortunately, bruvver also had a nasty bump on his head ('might knock a bit of sense into him' my mother said)...and the kind policeman advised that it should be 'seen to'.

I had this terrible urge to ask the Dayglo Mr Plod, whether he could take my dickhead brother BACK into town....but thought better of it.

A quick phone call to my Brother-in-law, and at 8.30am it was all systems go, and all of our respective Pre Christmas arrangements were thrown into disarray.

A while later I realised there was something dreadfully wrong with my eye(s)----and whatever it was would not desist, so I took the 'local yokel stagecoach' into the metropolis to see if I could get it fixed.

Two Hours after the other two members of my family had laid siege to the casualty department, I shuffled into THE WRONG SECTION of the hospital.

Obviously my sight was so impaired, I couldn't correct the country bumpkin cabbie (who kept bloomin' asking me 'you havin' a good Christmas?') who deposited me at some entrance with a wave and point of his hand.

'I can't SEE' I whined for emphasis.

Finally, I got to registration, and thank Christ she didn't just say: 'take a seat and fill in this form'...otherwise I would have written the legend: 'I cannot ****ing well SEE' on A5 paper and strapped it to my chest.

'Surname' she asked.

Now my surname is pretty rare, so when I told her, there was a slight hesitation.

'No' I pre-empted 'that was my brother a while a go'

With the form finally completed, it was phase two of: 'HOW CAN I CONVEY TO THE STOIC, SEEN IT ALL BEFORE, DISPASSIONATE STAFF----THAT I AM THE ONLY PERSON OF THE 50 SOULS WAITING WHO SHOULD BE FAST TRACKED TO SEE A DOCTOR IMMEDIATELY.

I convinced her that acid, or something of a phosphorous like corrosive agent was burning my cornea/retina and that the future of my eyesight depended on expedience.

I only waited 45 min, as opposed to the 3 hour projected time wait. I know police do the 'good cop---bad cop' routine, but this was 'good, soothing bedside manner to the Butcher from Rajasthan'

Informing me that I had a badly torn cornea in both eyes, he yanked my head back like a horse doctor, cruelly jammed some shit that made it sting 10 times as much, bandaged me up like the Pudsey, the 'children in need' mascot, and dispatched me on my less than merry way with: 'go to sleep and rest your eyes'.

Ha! Fat chance.....

Back home, my Mother was STILL determined to enjoy CHRISTMAS.

As a dutiful daughter, I offered to help wrap her presents....and was gently chastised for not putting the Sellotape in the correct place.

ILLNESS IS NOT ALLOWED AT CRIMBLE TIME

Crikey, this little Norfolk dumpling of a village hadn't had so much fodder for idle gossip (squad cars, paramedics and sighting of the Letitcia Black sheep) since the head teacher ran away with the dinner lady!!!!

That was Dec 2005.

Now in December 2006, emerging (escaping) with relief, I made the tortuous rail journey home (with, the ubiquitous engineering works on the line) and concurred with my fellow travellers, as I heard them tell their mates: 'I'm tellin' ya, another day an' I would 'ave bloody killed someone, it wuz doin' my nut in…..meet ya down the boozer then Bro'

Yes, these people had a jolly New Year to look forward to, while I was dangling at the mercy of a Governmental department who were determined to go as slowly as possible.

Still, it wasn't ALL bad, young Jason had emailed to request another appointment (all his Christmas money) in 2007, and I thanked a Higher being for small tender mercies………

KEEP YOUR FLOWERS, JUST GIMME THE MONEY

One of the traits, or rituals, I have inherited from my mother, is the 'softening of the soles' by immersion of feet into a bowl of soapy water.

This is done every day whilst I am creating, make up wise, the monster of my demise: LETITCIA, of Body Worship and Sex Goddess fame.

I knew I had hit mental -block bottom, when I stepped with one foot into the bowl….and then clear forgot what the next move was for 5 minutes.

This was the same mental state that had me walk 50 yards up the road--- WITH A SUPERMARKET BASKET FULL OF GOODS (TO THE VALUE OF £20-30) FOR WHICH I HAD SOMEHOW FORGOTTEN TO PAY.

Luckily, my mate Anya, an Employee of Threshers, noticed my lapse of concentration and laughingly pointed out my error.

'That's lovely new bag you have there' she said

I looked down and for a moment could not comprehend her statement. Then I squealed: 'OH MY GOD', and rushed back to the supermarket to admit my genuine mistake.

'I'm most terribly sorry' I gushed to a very perplexed member of staff, who it must be said, was not paid enough to give a shit.

Luckily there were enough staff members who had purchased my book, and liked me therefore it was laughed off as an honest mistake.

'Crap security men' I commented as I left.

I was going to have to cash in my 'Chemical Cosh' and start taking the very pills that I had so wanted to avoid.

My prescription for Anti-depressants was dog eared but ready for use, and I stopped off to admit defeat in the face of lunacy.

This lunacy, and panacea thereof, came at a whopping price.

'That will £27.50' said Trush, my friendly neighbourhood chemist.

I did a useful impersonation of my many phone enquires asking for the price of a 'penis polish'.

'HOW MUCH'? I shouted.

He repeated the price, and told me in fact he had given me 'a bit of a discount'.

'But one cannot AFFORD to be miserable!!!' I railed.

I took my pills home and stared at them. 'So, it's come to this eh' I said to myself, since talking to myself had also slipped into my demented daily life.

The easy slide into a vegetative state was moving apace. I found myself completing my make up…..just as the Sun was going down.

I found myself, for the first (only) time in my life not bothering with make up at all.

The last bastion was, the: 'What is the point of getting up?' question, though years of discipline would not allow me to do it.

I only managed a 1.Pm on a couple of distressed occasions, and I felt all the worse for it. Maybe there WAS something in the concept of Catholic Guilt

I hated my self-pity and wanted the hopeful, hedonist to emerge from the carnage.

'Bed sheet' emailed to ask for permission to submit my first Tax return in 30 years, exhorting me to print and return 'otherwise there will be a £100 penalty for a late Return'

Being under the Jack boot of the system was beginning to irk me. I had been so free and unfettered, blinded by ignorance, and (it seemed) paying a crazy price.

For comedic effect, 'Band Aid', who was steadily working on my personal injury claim emailed to ask: 'Could you tell me precisely what it is you do, and why, by virtue of your injuries, you feel you can no longer do it'.

Now, that question made me laugh. My reply was along the lines of: 'If you happen to know of any other way of administering fellatio (without kneeling) to my patrons, I would be very happy if you could let me know'.

Added to all this indignity was the approaching Bain of every sane person's life: Bloody Valentine's day!!!!

Luckily I had the perfect platform to vent my spleen. I was a columnist, albeit unpaid, and to a small local audience.....but I could talk about any cotton picking thing I liked.

I relished debunking the romantic love crap.

I wrote:

'Singapore Airport: clean, efficient, air-conditioned and welcoming to tourists of the world.

The city itself is much the same. No smoking, no chewing gum and god forbid if there is ever a Saturday night 'after Chinese banquet' bit of fisticuffs.

Being a clean, controlled and contained environment is great for the overseas visitor, but the inhabitants have a different view.

They long to break free from the tyranny of forced savings, and social engineering, It's illegal even, to partake in oral pleasure without culminating in penetration for goodness sake!!!!

But these issues aside, Lee Kwan Yew (retired prime minister extraordinaire) has done a stellar job at transforming a colonial outpost to a gleaming, high tech prosperous enclave, and I relished arriving for a bit of R&R from my domicile in Australia.

I always had Kelvin, my favourite handsome Male Escort, waiting (in full silk Malaysian national dress) just to start my mini holiday with a bang (doesn't everybody?) and once I flew there for Valentine's Day and the Chinese New Year.

We cabbed it from Changi Airport to The Dynasty Hotel, situated on a corner of the main thoroughfare: Orchard Road.

I dumped my bags in my salubrious premiere suite, and after a quick freshen up we decided to have a constitutional along the broad boulevard.

What an unedifying sight!!

We encountered an endless tsunami of flower carrying couples, in fact, a continual flow of brain dead lemmings.

The women look both content and smug.

The men, at best: looked sheepishly 'under the cosh', and at worst: 'pussy whipped'. They reminded me of the kiddie's donkeys being led along Hunstanton or Cromer Beach.

The women seemed satisfied and validated by making their current 'significant other' carry a bundle of blooms around the streets all day long.

The men (poor saps) went along with the spectacle because they knew hell on earth would be visiting if they did not Kow-Tow to the unspoken demands of the 'rittle rady'.

Not only did they have to make the ridiculous empty gesture, they had to be SEEN to be doing it as well.

What bollocks. And I thought this puke making spectacle was confined to Singapore alone.

Wrong.

Only last week, I eavesdropped on blokes in and around Brighton on the eve of the biggest fraud in the universe: 'Love to cum clubbin'...but y'know how it is bro'....if I don't do the full Monty on the day, I'm ****ed for the next year' or another conversation: 'No brainer mate, drinks wiv you lot and months of agro, or bite the bullet and do the lovey dovey shite wiv me bird for a quiet life' and a few other variations on that torrid theme.

So, like sheep, they did the dutiful thing by rote, and like their Singaporean counterparts, they embarrassingly got dragged around Brighton welded to their ball and chain.

I have opined many times: 'Love is a myth perpetrated by the makers of Hallmark cards and the proprietors of flower shops.'

There is only temporary lust/obsession/insanity, or the fear of being alone, with very little in between. It is a ridiculous form of human bondage

Economic necessity has more to do with couples shacking up than a grand passion, and the shared possessions, chattels and kids, are the glue that binds them together in a life of quiet desperation.

I have very fond memories of Valentines past, a spot of 'afternoon delight', punctuated by the hurried phone call to the WIFE explaining the delay in arriving to take her to dinner, and finally a proffered bundle of bank notes to support my lifestyle.

Well it works for me!!

It seems that ASDA was selling a dozen roses for two quid this year, well if women can be had that cheaply, they would do well to desist in calling me a cheap whore.

I'm not the kind of gal who swoons for a hastily purchased bunch of Garage Forecourt Chrysanthemums, and I don't want a rubber chicken meal with the rest of the grateful mules.

My men don't HAVE to say it with flowers (but they sometimes do) or make extravagant gestures proclaiming undying love (ditto) or feed me on one particular day…..they do it all year round.

Now THAT'S real and THAT'S love.'

The number of Kemptown Rag readers who actually AGREED with me was astonishing, and confirmed my long held view that the world is just going through the motions because they don't want to make a fuss.

My Valentine's Day was not without attention. A single rose from Bruce (Ex Patron) in Australia, with the accompanying card stating: 'Cheer up, it might never happen' and a withheld number on my mobile phone whispering: 'I'd LOVE to come over your tits'.

Yes, romance was not dead at all. My mind set though, was on another matter.

A FRIEND IN NEED IS A PAIN IN THE ARSE

Very few people stayed the distance with my personal set of problems. There were disgraceful lapses of communication from supposed mates, and where I had always been punctilious in answering phone calls or emails from them. Gradually I was given a wide berth. Changing from court jester to distraught pest seemed to test the mercurial nature of firm or supposed lifelong friendship

And then there was another breed entirely: HARRY, Essex Enigma, Wide boy and Artistic savant, who had fallen foul of my 'Turbo Sperm' practical joke.

The term 'ducking and diving' was made for him.

He continued to check on my un-well-fare.

He didn't so much speak, but launched forth into a tirade. He railed against injustice, harrumphed at hypocrisy and raged against the inept machine which was: Local or Central Government.

His spleen was so vented he required a weekly replacement

'This country is run by Wankers FOR Wankers' he pronounced in our last Mobile Phone interaction.

We commiserated with one another about the utter futility of attempting to sort ANY utility problem out----without either wanting to head butt the service provider spokesperson, or indeed the handset used to communicate with them.

'This world applauds mediocrity, it's all about form and no content, style over substance, AND' he paused for effect 'I fear that we as a Nation have become latent submissive proles'

Oh how I could have kissed this man.

He voiced the fear and concerns of all the bright citizens of the Island that used to rule the waves.

He could have given Hitler a run for his money in the demagogue list.

He was unashamedly bailing out and leaving the country. With paintbrush in one hand (he was selling his home) and a Mobile phone (which he had rescued from contract extinction, by some nifty talking on behalf of his 'bird') in the other, he waxed hysterical about the state of the nation.

When he paused for breath, he asked: 'OI, 'ow are the bleedin' Ladies of Llangollen'

He didn't swear because he lacked vocabulary, more because he had nowhere to put his grown up grumpiness and advanced adult angst.

'No news. Well, that is, other than the fact my file has been languishing at Crown Prosecution Service since I enjoyed my last wank'

'What does your brief say?' he demanded

I told him how 'The Whore whisperer' gleaned the information that the merging of Tax and Customs had rendered the HMRC 'in disarray' and therefore, for that and manifold reasons, they did not know how to proceed and needed to 'consult guidelines'.

'Yeah', Harry spat, that's 'cos they don't have a bleedin' MANUAL for it---they can't fuckin' think for themselves, they need a book to tell 'em what to do'.

Ah yes, everything was a procedure, a protocol, and a guideline.

A lumbering Leviathan never did any nifty footwork, yet a fair few of the Directors of Public Prosecution seemed adept at sticking their dicks in womenfolk other than their wives.

I had read about these shenanigans on high with a wry smile.

Everyone has a dirty little secret, no matter how fancy the job title.

One former DPP, Sir Allan Green QC, was even caught kerb crawling in Kings Cross with tragic consequences for his family, namely in the form of his wife's suicide.

These were my judicators. It did not escape my notice that the wildly inflated amount which the Revenue demanded was EXACTLY the amount (I read THAT somewhere too) it cost to kit out a High court judge.

I was bloomin' being mugged to deck out some QC in Ermine, horse hair wig and silk gown!!!!

Harry was simultaneously amazed and amused.

'I'm tellin' ya, hypocritical plonkers with the 'do as we say –not as we do' code of ethics' he spat in disgust.

We chewed the fat of the land, denouncing the cavalier way in which Tax payers money was unspent.

'Harry, I will give you an example of the blatant waste of money given disproportionately to the undeserving' I said

'Go on' he prompted, with the air of a man about to hear an official secrets act.

But first, I meandered off the subject and talked about the swings and roundabouts of being a free spirit.

'Harry, I used to be 'door bitch' of an illegal (!) gambling casino/club in the China town district of Sydney, and I learned pretty quickly never to take more than twenty Aussie dollars to work, since the politicians denied all existence of gambling in N.S.W.

It turned out to be a nice little earner for the police who came to raid the joint.'

'Really?' asked Harry, sounding like he had stopped painting.

'Yes REALLY. They would take all of the money found on the premises, and since we, the employees, were not supposed to exist---they took OURS as well!!!!'

'Cor, you've had some life haven't ya?' he exclaimed

I had only worked part time, but gradually this turned into all of the time and with no respite to catch up on sleep and generally recharge the drained battery of vitality.

This overwork was not because of innate greed on my part, but the fact that many of the staff would simply not show up or ring 10 minutes before a shift to announce the 'excuse du jour'

The owners sussed out that I was always willing to 'help out' when these emergencies arrived, but naturally they (and the staff with a zero work ethic) came to take me for granted

'You know what Harry' I continued, 'it was not until I asked for compassionate leave, to visit a sick relative that I saw the trembling lower lip always got more than my chuffing STIFF upper lip!!!!'

The 'never complain nor explain' culture had given way to 'problem people' getting away with murder.

When my boss sighed and said: 'I could have done with a bit more notice' I finally saw the light.

Being nice, good, punctual, and having an unimpeachable code of conduct, was SIMPLY NOT REWARDED in this world.

I finally got round to the juicy gossip which Harry longed to hear.

'Guess what Harry, I read a particular post on a local forum and my blood boiled' was my preamble.

It read ...... 'I discovered a few days ago that Brighton & Hove Council spent over £3,000 on sending flowers to all the Mums in Brighton & Hove who receive benefits.

They used one of the most expensive flower shops in the City. I overheard the manager in the aforementioned shop telling a colleague he'd just received their cheque for delivering them all.

Glad to see the council aren't THAT short of money after all.'

The forum poster just happened to be a vague acquaintance in this one degree of separation kind of world.

Un ****ing believable!!!!

I replied on the forum:

'Never been a benefit receiving Mum (sniff) God, think of all the flowers and freebies I could have received. My life blueprint has gone disastrously askew..... I demand the same 'Noblesse oblige' for an Erotic service Provider in dire straits.....

This is blatant discrimination.......'

Harry swore a bit more, so I took up the slack in the form of intellectualising the crazy decision

'Oh mate, it's not my intention to delve into the right or wrongs of single motherhood and the resultant receipt of governmental benefit, the subject matter is too complex, hey, good luck to them…I would LOVE to get something for nothing, but first, someone in a position of 'liberal sweet doling', would have to see me as a worth recipient…..and that is NEVER going to happen'.

I thought of all the times in my life that I had no income and resisted the urge to seek help. It just meant that my frugal outlook had been supplanted by 100 people who knew how to work the system.

AND GOOD LUCK TO THEM TOO!!!!

If there was a system in place which encouraged felons, the feckless and the work shy, then one could hardly blame individuals for taking advantage.

'Now' I continued 'my mind has run riot and, because a precedent has been created by the council, I will fully expect to see: A recreation by cryogenics, through DNA recovery, of every person who does not HAVE a Mother or Father for these stupid, man made celebration days of the year. Ditto for all those who have lost beloved pets too! Let's send flowers to every woman who does not have a loved one on Valentines

My point being: WHY ONLY PEOPLE ON BENEFITS????'

Harry finally recovered from the shock of yet another risible decision by the mental mandarins, and joined in with the spirit of madness.

'Oi, I'd like a bleedin' pole dancer on my birthday and blow job at Christmas'

And he wasn't kidding.

'It's a vote catcher Harry……. I have read about two government initiatives, whereby the unemployed, or should that read unemployable----- can get free: Head massage, Body Massage, Make up, Tattoo removal, Piercing removal, manicure, pedicure and hair styling….all in the name of being a pigging lazy git'

Our sirocco wind of scorn was blasting big time…until Harry's battery ran out.

It was just as well, where maladministration was concerned we could have 'bunnied' all day long.

WHEN TWO WHORES COLLIDE

There is a curious notion that we wander lonely as a cloud looking for our soul mate, though I have renamed it on numerous occasions as: ASSHOLE MATE.

Desperation often blurs the line between 'the one' and the 'eminently unsuitable'

Then there is a third category. It is the 'DO NOT UNDER ANY CIRCUMSTANCES, NOT EVEN FOR A NANO SECOND, GO NEAR THIS HUMANOID'.

Where playing with fire was concerned, hell, just call me Icarus!!!

So it was. I was at a literary party, hoping to find a publisher mad enough to take me and my tome worthiness to their heaving bosom/hairy chest.

My subject matter (smut) and my tendency to write in a stream of unconscious like kind of way, was a monumental drawback.

I refused to be reined in, like Picasso would have DIED rather than paint a symmetrical face.

So it was (Dec 2006), with a migraine, an ear infection and a gammy knee that I worked the room of this smoke filled party.

My gracious host Clare was magnificent in the introduction stakes, but my infection blighted ears could not discern the name of the many publishers she was introducing me to.

She would give me a knowing inflection of her head and Mona Lisa smile when she thought I could 'do business' (publishing wise) with her many guests, but it was irritatingly all lost on me.

I was deaf. There was a wall of sound not unlike Phil Spector's (music producer of the Sixties).

I gave a few of my Body Worship Books to those who showed interest in the ramblings of a deaf desperado, though bending the knees to reach for them nearly saw me commit a 'pro faux pas', since once down, I very nearly unable to complete the act of getting UP again.

And then I saw him. He was only marginally wearing more make up than myself, and had the obligatory adoring waif under his arm, but I only had eyes for him.

The fact that I had no ears was only going to be a minor drawback........

His diminutive 'wifelet' showed no sign of the jealous and abrasive nature which most women employ when their men folk indulge in a serious spot of flirting.

Clare once again nodded furiously as if to say: 'Work it Baby, OWN it....'

Somehow, I actually heard her say: 'This is Sebastian, he is known as 'The Brothel Creeper', the man who has slept with a thousand prostitutes'.

OH MY GOD...this man was the only person who I had met, read, or seen, who actually GOT IT.

He actually understood the Whore/Customer dynamic in the nicest sense, and by implication, he GOT ME.

'But, I've read the article you wrote in The Observer....it was.....well, it was the most beautifully written LOVE LETTER to the sex workers of the world' I said breathlessly.

His Heathcliffesque coal black eyes shone with added intensity.

'Darling, you liked it?' he gasped

Like it? It was one of the most profound pieces of writing since The Prophet.

He thought that the 'whore fuck was the purest fuck of all' and that 'the WORST things in life were free'

What a bloke!

I left the party. I had met someone who was (I hoped) going to be of great importance to me and I hobbled down the stairs, having signed a copy of my book for him.

It read: 'Sebastian you bastard, you still owe me fifty quid'

Within hours we started to become email buddies:

'Greetings Sebastian, it was most clement meeting the man who wrote a very misunderstood open 'love letter' to woman kind........

I myself have to crack on with my day and gird up my flagging loins with a spot of 'Cock worship at 4.pm'....do think of me at this time.

Let us do something together soon!!!'

He replied:

'Well we must be communicating. I wrote you an email yesterday and then realised I had no place to send it. You must have read my mind.

It was a real honour to meet you at the party. Didn't we glamorise it? Weren't we electric eels in a pond of goldfish? Weren't we the real thing amongst the sea of respectability? In my romantic view a woman may be a prostitute and she may be a destitute but she can never be less than a lady.

So glad you understood the open love letter to womankind that was much misunderstood by women unkind.

I am going to spend Christmas with you (as in the book) and I am very excited about it. And then I shall be praising you so much to Clare that you will only be able to get your hat on with a shoe horn.

Let's meet in the New Year?

As Ever

Sebastian'

I felt this was going to be the start of something big, something was just so INEVITABLE about it. Like my unholy life had been all about this moment.

I was constantly thinking about him and our emails moved and quaked with 'meant to be' sprawled all over them.

One day I had just gotten rid of a pesky punter who was becoming bothersome and I emailed:

'Oh Sebastian, I have just endured a session with, what I adjudge to be, 'the bane of the Erotic service provider'.....namely: the customer who is smitten.

Smitten so deeply, that he kisses in enthusiastic Labrador fashion (up to the chin only)......the poor fellow.

I received CD's, flowers, and even a bottle of my favourite libation; Laurent Perrier Rose.......and with each gift, my heart truly sank........

That is when you know 'tis time to cut the poor lovelorn Lothario adrift'.

I simply want to shout (in the cruellest of fashion).....'This is the sex for sale industry, not a bleedin' dating agency'

This is my worst night- mwhaaaaaa

I would imagine a similar thing could happen in reverse where your elegant self is concerned?????'

He replied:

'It is just so unprofessional of them isn't it? What do they take you for, The Millionaire of love'?

He sent photos of himself looking the bee's knees in an Avant Guarde, Comme de Garcon Parisian fashion show. I threatened to let the train take the stain of my mobilised 'G. String juice' and I had an informal invitation to tea at Chez Horsley.

In the meantime I went web wandering to learn as much as I could about my man.

I had somehow overlooked this important piece of a fucked finding mission.

Oh Dear. Oh Deary Deary dear. Oh fucking dear.

He had submarine-like 'down periscopes and dive, dive dive' sloshed all over his tall frame.

If love's young dream was: Bisexuality, Heroin abuse, Suicide attempts and a spot of self crucifixion in the Philippines ----he was my man.

On the plus side he HAD written that:

'Income tax has made more liars out of the British people than prostitution'.

How could I argue with that? He was a genius incarnate.

I continued my assault on his sharpened senses:

'In a perfect world, I would be combining a trip to see Clare (with a publishing deal) my personal injury Lawyer 'Band Aid' (the law suit for Somerfield) and my Tax Lawyer 'The Whore Whisperer' (telling me good news)...along with the man who broke a thousand hearts/hymens: Mr Horsley.

Shall we try and punt for the week after next?

I have one or two Body Worship appointments which I must honour and a visit for sheer torture (lip plumping...to give me the ultimate cock sucking pout)

Please let me know which day would suit, and let us do a spot of civilised banter and Bollinger'

He replied:

'Well, yes, I really think we *should* start some rumours. But who is going to buy who?'

OOOOh Er.

This was it, chocks away. The diversion from the car crash of my life was a gift of providence.

This was the man who had told Kate Moss he was not remotely interested in her coming to his studio because 'her looks and her greed were ugly'.

And (in my deranged mind) he wanted ME.

Maybe there was a God after all............

WHERE THERE IS BLAME THERE IS A CLAIM

My class action against Somerfield slowly descended into a Brian Rix farce.

It was funny enough to have a lawyer enquire as to what my occupation was, and why I felt, with my sustained injury, that I could no longer do it---- but when he asked if there would be any patron willing to be 'interviewed' as to why they thought I was not fit for purpose, I nearly cried with disbelief.

Undeterred, I actually asked a few customers whether they would like to help me with my personal injury claim-----with predictable results.

I could hear their sphincter muscle doing the Salsa.

As I wrote in my book Body Worship: 'When a man pays for a professional, the dosh is actually 'fuck off' money. It relieves them of not only a weighty matter in their testicles, but the guilt inherent in getting rid of the woman that has just performed it.'

They pay for LEAVING rather COMING!!!!! Bearing that in mind, I started the fruitless task of looking for a likely lad to assist 'Band Aid'.

I didn't do well.

Several offered to write an anonymous letter on my behalf and I thanked them profusely, even though I was thinking: 'I could bloody well do that MYSELF!!'

So it was that I received a letter from a gentleman with impeccable manners and breeding (himself a Magistrate).

It stated: 'I have been seeing Letitcia for some time, though less and less recently. The reason being, I am very traditional where my lovemaking is concerned, and I don't feel content unless I: a) Have intercourse and: b) have oral in a particular position.

I was disappointed when Letitcia withdrew penetration as a service, but she obviously had her reasons and her service was still of the highest standard. Now it appears she has difficulty in kneeling to provide Oral relief.

We did indeed try a different position for that particular manoeuvre, but since I myself have an injured hip, this also failed to be a success.

We did laugh about it, but, although Letitcia is a wonderful person, I feel paying £200 for a jolly good laugh is a tad steep and I can no longer justify spending money on a service I no longer receive.

I can imagine other customers would also find Letitcia's obvious discomfort off putting.

I trust you find this helpful.'

The letter encapsulated the (not unfair) selfish nature of men where sex, paying or otherwise was concerned.

Food analogies usually work where sex is concerned, and paying premium rate for a slap up Sunday Roast----only to be served with a soggy Yorkshire Pudding and zero gravy would be justifiably met with derision.

The reticence to help on the part of my punters was annoyingly understandable, yet immensely frustrating.

One customer replied:

'You have never done me any favours, yet you expect me to help you.'

It was tempting to reply with a scathing account of the number of times he had in fact paid less than the going rate, due to his wallet ALWAYS holding at least £10 less than was required.

I was also tempted to remind him that his turquoise ceremonial Free Mason's apron was not in fact meant to be used as a 'fetish uniform' in a normal Body Worship appointment.

His attitude was indicative of the 'do not give a shit about a tart in need' which many punters favoured. He did not want to help

Then there was the 'run for the hills brigade' who were too frightened.

The fact that they thought they were actually breaking the law was one factor. They were cruelly disappointed in their ignorance of the sexual statute book.

They WANTED to be bad!!!!

They needed one act of defiance which made them feel better about a timid unfulfilled life. They could NOT however, rebel enough to help me. They were rebels without a clue and born to be extra mild.

They could happily stand up in my cunt, but not in court.

Therefore, a spot of personal Basil Fawlty irreverence was required.

I decided to have a: BE AS NON COOPERATIVE AS POSSIBLE TO TELEPHONE ENQUIRES WEEK.

I had only done this once before in my life...and it was immensely satisfying, childish, but satisfying nonetheless.

When once an Aussie patron asked me in lascivious fashion: 'What would you like me to do with ya Sheila?' (yes, they really DO talk like that), I replied quite truthfully: 'I would like you to give me $A 220 and then FUCK OFF!!!!

He thought I was joking......... but I had never been more serious in my life.

This was how my week of irreverence went:

1) 'Letitcia, where do I park my car?'

My response: 'Side of the road pal'

2) 'Can I stick my cock up your arse?'

My response: 'Sure, only if I can return the favour with a dildo of the same size'

3) 'What do you do?'
My response: 'The very best I can'
4) 'Can I come 3 times?'
My response: 'Dunno, CAN you?'
5) How OLD are you, if you don't mind me askin'?'
My response: 'I was born the year they invented the teabag'
6) 'What can I get for £50?'
My response: 'A clip round the ear'
7) 'Can I have unprotected sex?'
My response: 'Sure, I will throw my (secreted under the mattress) baseball bat away'
8) 'I have a disability, would that be a problem?'
My response: 'Yes, it would…go and whine to someone else'
9) 'How much do you charge?'
My response: 'Like a wounded bull'
And so it went.

The natural masochists even made appointments and were subjected to a rudeness I had never unleashed….no matter what the situation.

'Can I use the bathroom?'

'Oh NO, that's extra' I quipped…..and they actually paid me to take a toilet trip

And the not unusual request of: 'Will you put suspenders and seamed stocking on for me?' heard me saying 'you'll get what you are given'

And they, the paying customer, actually took it.

I was a vile harridan and it took more energy to be ambivalent and provide a cursory service than to be my normal sweet self…… let alone to provide a mission statement of excellence.

I was a little ashamed, but hell, a lifetime of being acquiescent was driving me mad. I didn't want to be offensive, but I was tired of the sexual equivalent of: 'Doors to manual, chocks away,…..Coffee tea or me?……..can I get you a drink………enjoying your flight…..thank you for flying Letitcia Airways'

The price of appearing perennially happy was just too high where acting under extreme pressure was concerned. As most luvvies would ask of their director: 'What's my motivation daaaaaarling?'

I turned my attentions back to Sebastian, the undisputed King of Debauchery……

THE BEST LAID PLANS OF PRICE AND PEN

I thought that I should read a bit more about my current fantasy lover, and the Web offered up all kinds of information.

I read some more of his Blog, and wondered why his girlfriend Rachel called him 'Syph Boy'…and then I read on.

Bugger!!!!

There, in a few paragraphs, writ large was the Jonah of my future love life. He wrote with undisguised pleasure:

'Wonderful News, I've got syphilis!

I simply can't believe it. I never thought anything that exciting ever happened to me.

It started with a small red spot on my right arm. Within days my entire body had gone into revolt. My chest became blistered with a crimson rash. The red welts began to glow and throb. My torso had completely blown up! It looked as though hundreds of pairs of fuller figured jelly-fish were fornicating all over it. After a week some of the redness began to subside and the places where it had been to dry and harden into white scales. It was not a pretty sight. Oh my God, look at me! His and herpes!

I have to say I don't really believe in illness. I'd show up for work if my knob fell off. But even *I* was a little concerned'.

This information called into question just HOW cutting edge or wild I REALLY was. Immediately I knew I was a 'puddy tat' who pretended to be mad bad and dangerous to know.

I mean, a touch of thrush, maybe.

A bit of Non Specific Urethretis, okay.

But mother fucking hell. The disease of Kings and a 10 on the raddled Richter scale???

No way.

I Google searched the word 'Syphilis'. It made depressing reading:

'Painless sores or open, wet ulcers—chancres—often appear from three weeks to 90 days after infection. They last three to six weeks. They appear on the genitals, in the vagina, on the cervix, lips, mouth, or anus. Swollen glands may also occur during the primary phase'.

I was absolutely not going to engage.

I guess I was not hip hop and happening after all.

I had an unblemished tush like track record and I was loath to besmirch it---even for one of the most unusual and original men I had ever met.

I never heard a sonnet that went:

'How do I love thee, let me count the sores'

Nor a song that went:

'Shot through the heart, and you're to blame, baby you give chancres a bad name'

Even Sinatra never sang:

'Wet ulcers, I've had a few…..but then again too few to mention'

It was never going to fly

My Bird of Paradise had morphed into a DODO

'Back to the whoring board' as he would say.

I hoped that he had enough glorious creatures to service for the foreseeable 50 years and that he wouldn't notice that I was not responding to phone calls and emails.

YEAR (FOR THE DERANGED) OF LIVING DANGEROUSLY

Another useless Bank Holiday loomed, and it coincided with the anniversary of the letter of doom from the HMRC.

One WHOLE YEAR (2007)!!!!

When you make it past 50 you are on a slippery slope to a 'y' shaped box and a future of worms crawling around your eye sockets and poo hole.

And what did I do with this gift of life? Worry.

I worried all day and every day about seeing a letter poking out of my mail box, hearing a new message arrive in my email, the ring of the telephone, the slightest sound at night.

I did suggest to the 'Whore Whisperer' (not for the first time) that I couldn't take it any more, but it appeared there was no statute of limitations (time wise) on the unimagined mental horror Governmental departments were prepared to meter out to perceived miscreants of the realm.

Adding mind boggling injury to insult, it appeared the Taxation department had decided to issue an extremely covert and back handed AMNESTY for uncollected taxes, though this seemed to apply to white middle aged MEN.

I queried this with 'Bed Sheet' and he disclosed that: 'the sly old chaps at the Revenue have not been completely upfront about it.'

I asked the 'Whore Whisperer', who was a little more expansive by explaining: 'As you have already been the subject of an investigation and made disclosure I do not think that technically you meet the criteria but I am tempted by the idea - if only to confront the Revenue with the inconsistencies in their approach. If you hadn't paid millions of pounds in tax they would deal with you civilly. They are now offering amnesties to people who have made deliberate and concerted efforts to hide money from the Revenue. You simply have not filed returns in respect of relatively small amounts and face possible criminal prosecution! You couldn't make it up!'

Yes indeed.

I had previously enjoyed a night at the theatre watching Rik Mayall in his spookily precise invention and satire: Alan B'stard.

The show pointed out the anomalies and vagaries of Government, the 'Do as we say, not as we do' drone of the elected/appointed brain dead, self-serving fuckwits.

It highlighted the merciless behemoth bearing very slowly on my beleaguered head.

In fact, I had spent my last £27 on trying to smile. I faced an Easter

Weekend with no money. 'Tips had been a bit light' as they say. I had received no 'gentlemen callers' for about 3 weeks, and the annoying 'grockles' from out of town were about to invade with their screaming unruly sprogs and their litter dropping ways.

The next day, I fished an empty wine bottle from my rubbish bin and presented it to my local off license as: 'Corked', as apologetically as a guilty, impecunious, 'down on her luck' prossie could act, though no acting was necessary.

Over the weekend I saw families enjoying glorious sunshine and the freedom an uninterrupted coastline seems to offer.

Crazed by hunger and a sense of futility, I did something I had NEVER done in my 15 years' tenure. I walked down to the seafront and sat watching the waves lap onto the shore.

It grew dark but I didn't care about personal safety. I didn't care at all about ANYTHING. I wanted to walk into the sea and disappear.

I heard the crunch of feet on stones approaching.

'Fuck off' I thought.

As anticipated, the crunching sound stopped and the weight of the person plopped down beside me.

'Fuck off' I thought more desperately.

The person asked: 'you aw'right?'

I turned to see a post-menopausal woman's security nightmare.

The suspect was: Male, Caucasian, a tall streak of piss (as in six foot plus) and smelt of the 'fag fog' which comes of standing in a bar/club for hours. I couldn't see his face since he wore the bad ass-just gotten out of jail look, favoured by youngsters who had not fully developed a character or fashion sense of their own.

'Huh?' I replied. I didn't wish to encourage him.

He told me I had in fact been crying. 'Does me 'ead in to 'ear a lady in distress' he explained.

He removed his 'Hoodie' to reveal the face of an Angel...... albeit with an unsettlingly attractive 'boxer's nose'

My normal seduction technique was stifled by my urge to sob uncontrollably for another hour or so.

I don't remember how we stumbled along to the subject, but, he seemed to have 'discovered' a great band called 'Deep Purple' who, apparently were playing Brighton later in the month.

I gently provided the info on the illustrious career of one of my favourite bands, thus illustrating the age gap of fellow sea shore gazers.

As he walked me home, such burning issues as the best 'axe man' in the Rock scene or the best workable rides (surfing wise) were discussed.

The inevitable Cunnilingus question reared its head in the form of; 'I can't find a bird who will let me do it' (who ARE these stupid women?)

I tussled for all of 2 seconds with the thought that I might bestow Noblesse Oblige on this poor unfortunate Oral Sex Maniac.

Hell, I was going to have my bits of happiness (and NOT crappiness) where I could.

According to the American constitution, we should not expect it (happiness) but the PURSUIT of it is written literally in stone.

At 18 years old, he was the perfect fraction, as in, he could go three times into me (or rather my age).

We dispensed with formalities and got straight down to a most clement tongue lashing.

This, young man had perfected the art of tracing the letters of the Alphabet with his tongue.

By the time he got to 'C' I knew I was onto a winner.

Tony Blair may have felt the 'Hand of History' on his Shoulder as he signed the Good Friday Agreement many moons before.

What I was feeling, though not worthy of column inches, was in another part of the anatomy and ten times more exiting.

Ten minutes earlier I was sobbing, and now I was moaning with delicious pleasure.

Funny old world, you never know what's round the corner.............

Harry threw back his head and laughed expansively when informed of my last sexual escapade.

'Oi, Letitcia, David Cameron said we should: 'HUG a Hoodie' not bleedin' 'HUMP a Hoodie'....'ow old was the young man?'

'Eighteen'

This information elicited more expansive laughter.

'You don' arf like 'em young you Cradle Snatcher'.

I needed to point out a salient issue.

'Harry, it is less me reaching into the cradle and more them pole vaulting over the bugger to get to ME!!!!'

We discussed what was surely going to be my looming bankruptcy.

'Had much work?' he enquired

'Nope'

'What are you going to do?'

'Dunno'

We looked at each other, and simultaneously had a funny thought.

Harry verbalised it first: 'You could always ask for yer bleedin' job back at the Tax office'

OH HOW WE LAUGHED.

GOVERNMENTAL SPONSORED RENDITION

Tick followed tock, night and day of anguish and fear ensued. I had outlasted a member of the Crown prosecution service (who was dealing with my case), and thus, my torment was prolonged.

WW, my long suffering brief, advised me to catalogue the mental and physical problems that had manifested themselves in the time since the entire imbroglio had kicked off.

From a sense of innate pride, I emailed back to him that I never thought the disabilities (of the defendant) written about in the national newspapers (where a criminal prosecution was imminent) were real, and that frankly it was beneath me to 'play' the 'pathetic card'.

The reality was that I was in danger of a stroke.

Medical evidence was duly supplied, only for the oracle: CPS/HMRC to reject the frivolous notion of calling off the prosecution....because my physical/mental demise was not deemed of a serious nature!!!

'I guess you have to top yourself to get them to sit up and notice then WW'? I spat.

The year of 2007 gently glided along until the first magistrate court appearance beckoned.

I was reliably informed by WW: 'Even murderers start here'.

Julie Burchill demand to accompany me to this first foray into the legal unknown.

This was very kind, but there was nothing more traumatic involved other than having to duly confirm my name and address.

The next date with legal beagles (re-scheduled after a court usher failed to understand there are not 31 days in November) escalated from sitting on a bench in full view of the magistrates to being ushered (VERY much against my will) to a bullet proof (presumably) cage where I was guarded by a court heavy.

EEEeekkk!!

Having (over a disgraceful amount of time) slid gently into the arms of the HMRC, I was now on a fast moving Cresta run to the hard yard. Yep, Crown court here I come.

WW, my solicitor, had engaged the services of 'Slide Boi' (Sliding down a Barrister, geddit??) who was a charismatic, enthusiastic Labrador of a man. Months previously I had congratulated WW on his ability to find the one man in London that I had not sucked.

Slide Boi when he arrived at Hove Crown court was bewigged and gowned to such a degree that I nearly failed to recognise him myself.

I was informed that this is the whole point of Judges and Barristers 'hiding' their real identity. Some defendants can get JOLLY batey (when banged up by the afore-mentioned), and therefore, a certain physical obfuscation becomes necessary.

Apparently, after the hearing (where I pleaded an emphatic: 'not guilty'), the Judge commented to Slide Boi: 'How very, very nice to see haute couture in court'.

This whole gig was becoming greatly educational.

A date, for my 3 day trial was vaguely set for May 2008.

In the interim period some very weird things started to happen.

The 'Anus' ran an item (in Dec 2007) where it curiously stated that I wore a 'Haute Couture Hat' (!!!!!!) and that I owed a chuffing amount THREE/FOUR times the actual debt, which was clearly the hyper inflated extrapolation of which HMRC is so fond. Why let the truth get in the way of a good prosecution,.......just pick a number and quadruple it seems to be plan a) b) and c) of the Criminal investigation's manual.

A whole 6 weeks later, this figure, along with my name and age was headline news on the hour every hour for BBC Southern counties radio. I couldn't work out if it had been a slow news day (the first item was the news of unexplained deaths at Deepcut Barracks!) or if suddenly the HMRC machine was moving to extract maximum exposure to the fact they were going to shaft me into the middle of next week. If I was being made an example then it flew in the face of every protocol stated on their website, and in their own guidebook. They REALLY had a hard on for me!!!

Harry (in one of his weekly phone calls) scoffed: 'Ow much is this bleedin' costing the taxpayers of this nation?' 'Yes' I replied gently 'I know, but you cannot expect a Tax collector to actually COLLECT it, can you, they have to SPEND it on putting the Sex industry on high alert!'

It really was quite galling to be used as a poster girl for their ambitions (they thought they had a big fish to fry) when in the tax food chain I was a mere minnow.

I wished the next few months of my miserable life away. The Two year mark of the very first missive from my adversary came and went, along with the proposed 3 day trial date (Bed Sheet was on maternity duty)......and my very own Lawyer, WW, had a job offer too good to miss.

'Distraught' as an adjective hardly did my feelings justice.

Harry merely said: 'Rats always leave a sinking ship'...........

THE TAXMAN CUMMETH

The morning of my 3 day trial arrived (June 2008). I checked for messages on my computer (stay of execution maybe?) 'Vitriol and Violets', as promised, had booked his holiday to coincide with my demise, and was part of the small team I had giving me wonder-bra type support. Julie Burchill was (of all things) my character witness. There was previous discussion among my legal team as to whether a woman who had (in a national newspaper) been branded 'The worst mother in Britain' and who had a reputation for a nefarious lifestyle would be the best person to back me up, but I thought, since I was not exactly Mother Teresa, it was very fitting. She was an unwavering friend who went the distance with me.

As it happens, The Taxman got a resounding spanking.

Never did I think that I would stand in a Crown court, surrounded by prosecuting/defence counsel, Judge and Jury and say the words: D*CK, F*CK, AND C*NT. (True)

You would be forgiven for thinking: 'Now is not the time to acquire Tourette's syndrome possum!!!'

But I did.

Never did I think that my good friend Julie Burchill would skip colt-like, up to the witness stand, with her skirt tucked in her knickers. (True)

But she did.

Being, as I was, enclosed behind glass, 'avec' Guard, I thought it ill behoved me to rap on my cage and shout: 'Oi, Scamp (my nickname for her), too much information!!'

She did much later explain in an email: 'The thing about that skirt is that it wasn't tucked in, but because I have such a big aye-uss it rides up when I sit down. Then, when I stand up, it doesn't return!'

You would think, seeing as we went to the same gym, a spot of pre trial derriere reduction would have been in order, but, on the first day of my trial, OUR GYM BURNED DOWN!!!

'It's a sign Julie' I commented 'Like a burning bush'

Elsewhere, 'Team Letitcia' seemed a pretty impressive bunch where honed buttocks of the walnut cracking variety were concerned. 'Bed Sheet' (Accountant) regularly slings himself down mountain tracks on his 53 gear Shimano 'Rock Hopper' bike, 'Beagle Baby' (Paralegal) was not OLD enough to acquire a gross 'gluteus mega maximus' and 'Slide Boi' (Barrister) cuts a dash, a-la –Tour- de France, with his macho 'Condor' racing bike through the thoroughfares of London.

Yes, my guys were well fit!!!

They were also, (unlike certain sections of government), 'fit for purpose'--- for against all odds ('They win most of their prosecutions' I had been told), I CHUFFING WELL WON!!!

Even if the general public is not up to speed where litigation is concerned, the first and only rule of thumb is: IGNORANCE IS NO DEFENCE IN A COURT OF LAW.

Yes, you guessed it-- that WAS my defence.

HOWEVER, there is one exception to that rule. That being: IF YOU ARE A SEX WORKER WHO DOES NOT KNOW ABOUT THE TAX LIABILITY, THEN IGNORANCE IS ACCEPTED, (information supplied by an Ex Tax Inspector).

God bless being a strumpet!!!!

Back to Crown Court's moments of levity, in a sea of fear and loathing.

Prior to our arrival in court, my 'Team Letitcia' and also my crew of well-wishers and supporters were like naughty school children swapping Pokemans or football cards. My legal teams' Business cards were given to my mates on the prompt of: 'Never know when we might need you guys', Julie did an impromptu book signing of her myriad literary feats and dispensed the same like lady bountiful to everyone. Igor got a booking to do his 'celeb personal shopping' with Julie (which is why he was there in the first place), while 'Slide Boi' wondered aloud if she (Julie) minded reading the first three chapters of his fledgling children's book.

I for once, sat like a spare pr*ck at a wedding while the wheels of contra deals and networking were spinning.

We waited in the corridor as the opposition arrived en masse.

'Which one is 'Frick' asked 'Vitriol and Violets', I gestured to my nemesis and he commented: 'Somebody did not sleep well last night'

I was heartened to see that she looked like me. Haunted, careworn, crazed.

Prior to sloping into court, we read the headlines of my trial as reported by the Argus for the previous day: TAXING TIME FOR BRIGHTON SEX STAR. As is usual in these cases, they found an archived picture of Moi which made the famous mug shot of Myra Hindly seem alluring. Then very helpfully beneath the photo, they stated: 'Can often be spotted in St James's Street, Brighton' (duh), like I was some near extinct species of the great breasted, lesser spotted curlew.

Due to the length of time required to sit in the dock, I had asked that certain medical conditions be taken into consideration, but, cometh the hour, cometh the 'twelve angry men' and (who knows?) a hanging judge, these entreaties seemed to go astray.

My Diverticulitis made it a painful time in an enclosed penal pen without 'comfort breaks'.

I eventually had to nudge my guard away from his 'Take a Break' crossword puzzle so that he might convey to my team that, quite frankly, I was in agony with a bursting bladder.

The whisper went to my 'Beagle Baby' and 'Slide Boi' was given a written note to the effect that his defendant was liable to p*ss herself if the court was not adjourned for 10 minutes.

'Slide Boi' then passed a note back to 'Beagle Baby' who passed it back to my diligent guard, who told me I HAD TO FREAKING WELL HANG ON!!! What a sadist!!

It seems on a point of law, he (Slide Boi) was on a roll, and if one's magnificent 'main man' is 'in the zone', the only thing to do is SUFFER like a good'n.

After twenty minutes of abject misery, I was just about to grab a polystyrene cup sitting idle in the dock-- and shove it up my palazzo pants for a covert emergency operation (the guard being in intense concentration over 3 down and 5 across)) when divine intervention in the form of concerns that THE JURY MIGHT NEED A CIGARETTE BREAK, gave me my most satisfying bout of urination (at the Ladies toilet) in my scar studded life.

As for the attendant panic attacks and defibrillation, I maxed out on the Bach Flower rescue remedy kindly donated by Julie (though Laurent Perrier Rose would have been better), and did the kind of deep breathing exercises expectant mothers are encouraged to do.

My mate Vitriol and Violets (who, not only was in court but carried my heavy trial papers each day) opined that he would never again pay go to the theatre.

'Why is that?' I asked.

'Because' he replied 'There will never be anything else that has this much drama'....he then paused for effect, and whispered menacingly in my ear 'And, If you do not need to use these heavy papers and appointment books, which I have been lugging around for last three days, I suggest you ring 'ARSEHOLES R US' because you luv, are going to be needing a new one!!

A moment of levity was much welcomed, though, as it happens I DID indeed need my appointment books on the last day under (very) cross examination by the prosecution.

He (HMRC Barrister) picked them up, between thumb and forefinger, with a withering look of distaste on his pinched badger like features, as if there was still some imaginary fresh jizzum besmirching the stiff leather binds.

He wanted to know what the letters CBFM and MOBY signified when written against a patron's name.

There was nothing for it, I was going to have to swear and make myself look crude and un-lady like which indubitably was what he wanted.

'Er' I started cautiously, wondering if 'Slide Boi' would give an inkling, via a raised eyebrow as to whether this was a good idea 'CBFM' is an acronym for a phrase that I picked up in Australia'

'Mr Badger', honed in on my obvious discomfort and asked me to spell out the words, which just happened to be 'CUNT, BITCH, FUCK, MOLE'.

I went on to explain that it was an Oz colloquialism, used when the person swearing the words was under extreme duress, frustration or provocation.

In my case, I used them to denote that some invertebrate with zero manners had booked an appointment and then not bothered to present themselves.

'And the word: 'Moby'?

I explained further that the Moby word in question was short for Moby DICK, and this meant that a particular enquiry (from a potential booking) had not left me with the feeling that I would like to spend one minute, let alone sixty, in the company of this person.

So, Vitriol and Violets would not need to annihilate my anus after all.

Later on, the tears flowed. I was determined not to do the 'big girl's blouse' scenario, but, when, on the witness stand I finally realised that instead of doing something I enjoyed, that I might be MADE to do it by my opponents (so that I might stand a chance of paying my tax bill) this lady turned lachrymose.

Being trafficked or pimped is an untenable and unreasonable situation, and, to that end I had decided, due to the stress and anxiety of the case, to give up 'trading'. The sheer amount of time that Crown Prosecution (or whoever) took to bring the farrago to trial meant that there was nothing left in the pot.

I conveyed those feelings to my jury of peers.

I reasoned with the analogy: 'You wouldn't put David Beckham on the pitch with a broken foot, much less Tiger Woods on the golf course with a broken arm'

Come the last day, the summations of Prosecution and the (although I say it myself) masterful defence of Slide Boi, concluded by the (wise) Honourable Judge meant that we had arrived at the moment of truth.

Within the time it took Slide Boi to suck on a crafty fag (!!!!!), the verdict was in.

EEEEEeeeek!! What did that MEAN??

My knees turned to jelly and my heart turned to an alarming drum solo.

'Pig's d*ck' I thought 'two and a half years, and I am going to have a bleedin' heart attack before I finally reach the end' They really should install defibrillation units at all Crown courts.

I stand up, the jury march in, and I cannot bear to glance in their direction for a sign.

The clerk asks if they have reached a unanimous decision (they had) and the foreman of the jury then says the sweetest words in the lexicon of life (other than 'I have a twelve inch tongue and have just won the Lottery'): 'NOT GUILTY'........

I heard the sound of a wounded animal and found in fact that it was me, sobbing with the anguish of immense torment being finally dissipated.

I limped away in a distressed state BEFORE the Judge's comments post verdict, though I can tell you this: HMRC's team got a bollocking, for, yes, you guessed it: WASTING TAXPAYER'S MONEY!!!!

You truly could not make it up......

Vitriol and Violets strutted out of court and with a glint in his eye (were they tears?) and pronounced: 'It is gannae be a long wee trip back to Wales for that 'Frick'!

Although in a state of extreme anguish, I phoned the person who had been my salvation: 'The Whore Whisperer'. Croaking with emotion, I exclaimed in all seriousness: 'I have won...and I would gladly drink your bath water!!'

With exquisite comic timing, he informed me: 'I am so happy for you, but really, that will not be necessary!'

Post acquittal, the Anus's headline was (at its dreadful finest): 'HOOKER DODGES TAX FRAUD CHARGES'.

Why did they not go the whole hog (and as usual, make it up as they go along) and write: DOMINATRIX FLOGS HMRC'S BIG AYE-USS TO A PULP.

(Illegal as it happens).......

I had (I believe) achieved a legal precedent.

One day later I received a congratulatory email from WW's replacement 'Seaman-San'.

His final words were most prescient:

'HMRC ARE NOTORIOUS LOSERS'

If HMRC were a blow job, it would be determined not to have a 'happy ending'........

AND THE HITS JUST KEEP ON COMING!

The calm in the eye of this litigious cyclone, was, as anticipated, very short lived.

I was a battered and bloodied prize prossie fighter, who had barely beaten the count, before my relentless opponent started pummelling me with renewed vigour.

There was no time for a sense of self-congratulation at my 'David' slaying their 'Goliath'.

Rising at 5.30 am on the day after the trial, I tried to get on with the rest of my life.

The pent up emotions of the previous years had other ideas. I was mentally shot. This uncoiled spring paced for hours trying to unravel the anguish, anxiety and horror of what had gone before.

This state of utter 'meltdown' was punctuated by the arrival of a well-wisher, who had bought balloons, flowers and words of warm encouragement.

Beautiful people such as this were willing me to stay strong and present a victorious front.

The next day, after more unravelling of the tense spring, I rang my 'voice of reason': HARRY.

As usual, he was in his element where effing and blinding the curse of the Government, and especially where the 'beaten assailant' was concerned. Momentarily, he also, could not understand my lack of jubilation.

'But Harry' I sobbed 'does NOBODY understand, I haven't won ANYTHING, I have no customers, no job, no income and the bastards are going to come after me with relish'.

He got it.

My life, rather than my sphincter, was buggered.

In no particular order, within a month of my acquittal, the following things occurred.

1) The Argus decided to kowtow to some meddlesome press body and stop all massage, (but let us not kid ourselves), hell let us face it,:- all prostitutes' adverts. The bread and butter of my earnings were being erased in one fell stroke. This, after years of accepting our (sex workers') not unsubstantial 'grubby money', and yet making much of stories outing all salacious 'sex for sale' exposes. What Hypocrisy.

Bif- wham!

2) My managing agent made a thinly veiled threat/shot across my sagging bow, that I could face eviction for contravening some sub section of my lease (where embarking on a trade or profession from residential

premises). Some kind public spirited Drongo had sent the news clipping of the trial to the agent's Head Office.

Kerpow-bam!

3) HMRC decided to put my last tax return 'under investigation'. 'Bed Sheet' informed me: 'This could cost you thousands to defend'.

Zap- thank you man!

4) The local team from 'HMRC Debt management' sent (predictably) a Distraint order to seize my goods, blah blah, threat, yadda yadda. This letter (also predictably) thumped through my letter box on Christmas Eve.

Kerplunk!

Once again I resembled an impotent one legged arse kicker.

When was this all going to end?

I may have 'dodged' a bullet, but this was death by a thousand cuts.

By 2009 half the recovery offices of the UK seemed to have a real 'hard on' for me, in respect of the unpaid 'debt'.

No matter how many forms I filled, detailing my income (zero), savings (zero) amount I would like to pay (zero) assets (zero), they just didn't catch my drift.

The local office accepted my position and said they would not seek to recover the debt 'unless circumstances changed'.

I metaphorically stuck my head in the big bad lion's mouth and by phone enquired as to what circumstance would be deemed a 'change'.

The answer came: 'If you win the lottery'.

Therefore, when I continued to receive threatening missives, I yet again outlined my case and ended the letter with: 'I believe this concludes our correspondence since I have not as yet won the lottery'.

Letters from London were referred to letters I had written to Newcastle, who themselves had been referred to letters I had written to Taunton, who themselves had been referred to the (as I thought) final and definitive letter I had written to my local office.

Harry pointed out a flaw in my correspondence.

'Are you bleedin' dopey of somefink?'

'How do you mean' I asked.

'Every time you reply, it is just another piece of mail they have to pick up and look at to justify their sad scabby little existence,....just ignore them' was his learned advise.

So I did just that. There was a very pleasing lull before another almighty storm.

I was targeted by HMRC's designated 'Rottweilers', and by that I mean the state sponsored goons (Debt collectors) who demand money with menaces and with impunity.

After about the twentieth letter I gave up with detailed explanations and heartfelt pleas to the better side of their nature, it merely seemed to give them an even bigger hard on.

I did something I had never done before (and THAT is saying something).

I asked my local MP to go in to bat for me, and would you Adam and Eve it…..my file was pulled from the nasty men driving me even more insane. It seemed a letter on House of Commons headed note paper really concentrated the mind and made them sit up and take notice.

Another lull, and yet, sometime later, the London office (again) started up on this interminable charade.

Having been 'BROUGHT up', rather than 'DRAGGED up' I never once wrote what every fibre of my being wanted to state, and that was: 'WHICH PART OF 'I HAVE NO FREAKING MONEY' DO YOU NOT UNDERSTAND?'.

So, I took Harry's advice and wilfully ignored it.

They in turn replied within a week to state they were 'Very disappointed' that I had not responded to their computer generated demand.

Disappointed? I was livid to have lost 6 years of my life to this Kafka-esque farrago.

I was as mad as hell and I was not going to take it any more……..

AND NOW, THE END IS NEAR.....

I once read a fable about a little boy who was told not to go up to the mountain, because a fearsome giant with large fangs and sharp claws resided there. Said boy did what any other adventurous little boy would do, he decided to find out for himself what dangers lurked on high. The funny thing was, the closer he got to the summit, THE SMALLER THE GIANT APPEARED.

HMRC, the vexatious litigant, was, after all, a toothless dwarf masquerading as a fierce tiger, a hollow mockery of a sham of an enigma, a cold collation of maladministration and sadistic 'jobs-worth' souls.

Though, as Harry would say: 'Oi, 'o else would do that poxy job?'

Quite right Harry.......

Today, 6th Dec 2013, Nelson Mandela passed away. I mention this only because the South African authorities (back in the day) had hoped to make some political gain in incarcerating an individual they felt could be paraded as 'AN EXAMPLE'.

He felt, on his release from prison, that to harbour resentment would be like 'drinking poison and expecting the enemy to die'.

He actively preached forgiveness for the good of the nation and the world beyond, but, I am not that evolved as a human being..........

Were my title to be: Amazon, Starbucks, Vodaphone or Google, and an amount owing in Tax registered in the billions, I would have been courted assiduously by the director of HMRC (as has indubitably been the case with conglomerates owing billions) and had the entire amount written off and moved operations to another off shore location to minimise my liability.

I read today that although 'MPs like to attack' the aforementioned 'for not paying their taxes, they have yet to actually create legislation compelling them to do so'!

I do understand why they did it, for the likes of 'Frick and Frack' and the other witnesses for my prosecution were every bit as ignorant (and that was essentially my crime) than myself, and were hopelessly out of touch with the life of an Erotic service provider. And in 'Frick's' case, she was, it transpired in court, a 'lifer' having been in the employ of HMRC for (if memory serves) 30 years. Therefore, they are to be pitied rather than vilified and castigated.

It is a bit of a bugger to be the victim of (what I perceive to be) a malicious prosecution. I was the patsy, the fall guy, an 'acceptable loss' in the theatre of war. I am reliably informed that they are paid on 'performance'. They took a bit of a pasting with me!!!

Even uglier, is that the Government seem complicit in deliberately keeping collection of 'immoral earnings' as some dirty little secret (not a vote catcher obviously).

I was confident that the jury of my peers would not have had the faintest clue as to this 'arrangement'.

My sublime Barrister 'Slide Boi' pointed out in court that though I was expected to pay into the system, that same system would not formally recognise me as a 'business' per se.

I would not be able to register as a company, although, and here is the hypocrisy, were I to LIE, (as suggested by many accountants for sex workers to register as 'beauty therapists, nail technicians, massage/aroma therapists' that would be another matter.

Funnily enough, if I was a street walker illegally touting for 'trade' or a burglar, I would not be liable for the purposes of taxation as affairs are not arranged in such a way as to constitute a 'trade' or 'profession' !!!

The charge of 'knowing fraudulent Tax Evasion' (Section 144 Finance Act) is essentially about being dishonest and dishonourable.

I was (correctly) found not guilty and acquitted. The amount owing was a paltry £7,000. Somehow, I am bemused and nonplussed that although the Authorities were offered that amount, and more, back in 2006, they embarked upon a futile odyssey which would comfortably have cost the British Tax payer, (by my computations) a healthy six figure sum.

No wonder the British economy is in such a parlous state.

The incompetence and ineptness displayed by the Criminal prosecutors make it hard to wonder where on earth they would ever get another job in the real world and it defies credulity that any of the protagonists should have retained employment after the debacle of the case. But, as we are shown many times over: (Bankers, C.E.O's, Directors etc), mediocrity, nay, mind numbing MEGA monumental cock ups seem to be rewarded.

Somehow, I know what Harry would say today:

'YOU DOPEY BINT, YOU SHOULD HAVE IGNORED THE BLEEDIN' LETTER!!'

LESSONS MUST BE LEARNT (BUT RARELY ARE)

I am often lambasted for reading the 'Bigots' Charter': The Daily Mail.

But, of all the journalists (even though he does not appear to have a very healthy attitude to sex workers) 'LittleJohn' is the Dog's Gonads…

He highlights hypocrisy ad nauseum.

One of his oft quoted assertions is this: 'IF YOU GIVE A PERSON A MODICUM OF AUTHORITY AND POWER, THEY WILL ALWAYS, ALWAYS, ALWAYS ABUSE IT'

And lo, it came to pass……

In order to make a case such as my own, to show a spike on a 'target', or 'graph' for 'statistics' (as pointed out to me by my dear 'WW' at Crown Court) these employees of the 'Crown' are obviously given 'Carte Blanche' to fritter and fling away money willy nilly to make a headline.

'97p in the pound (expended to make a prosecution)' was the figure muted by the expensive consultant drafted in by 'Bed Sheet' (accountant).

Dear reader, YOU do the maths.

I fear there may be a certain megalomaniac 'God complex' inherent in throwing money at a problem (like the collection of Taxes) and I was just 'it' in their eyes.

They were just rich bullies.

Once these employees of HMRC were on the stand in court, my oh my, how the scales fell from my eyes. They seemed to 'out gibber' my own self as a gibbering, quivering wreck.

One of the most satisfying moments (for me) was watching Slide Boi cross examine 'Frick' from HMRC Criminal investigations. He fixed her with a gimlet eye and nonchalantly enquired: 'Do you happen to know the threshold for VAT?' Obviously she didn't, for the question hung in the air like a lap dancer's pole. 'I don't know' she meekly replied. He paused theatrically, crossed his arms and said in a leaden voice with just the correct amount of derision within: 'YOU DON'T KNOW'. She was invited to take a wild guess and took 'wild' to an entirely new level (somewhere between double and triple the amount as I recall). Attempting to gloss over her woeful lack of knowledge she asserted/snapped: 'I don't HAVE to know'.

WONDERFUL, I had a warm Weetabix glow over that one delicious piece of payback.

Another one of my tormenters visibly winced when on the stand, as he was forced to concede that there was in a fact an 'awareness campaign' that was being rolled out across the country to get the message out to Sex workers that they had to pay tax on their ill-gotten gains.

Bloomin' CHEEK!!

The whole point of my case was:

'You owe us/HMRC/the government tax on your earnings'

Me: 'Oh, really? I'm most terribly sorry, I did not know'

'Well you SHOULD know'

Me: 'Well, HOW would I know?'

'Well, you just SHOULD, and we think you knew'

Me: 'I did NOT!!'

'We KNOW you knew and it is up to you to prove otherwise'

So I DID. (Prove otherwise!)

Now, I found that HMRC knew that Service providers DIDN'T know, yet maintained that I SHOULD.

Another less than relishing example of discrimination and boorish judgmental behaviour came from another HMRC Muppet, whose name will forever be a swear word in my home.

While trying to extrapolate FIVE times the amount actually owed (and I think you will find that it is 'demanding money with menaces'), he allegedly insisted to 'Bed Sheet' (accountant): 'We think there is more', 'Bed Sheet' countered with: 'Well, where is it then?'...to which he slanderously replied in frustration: 'Look for all I know she earned it and shoved it up her nose'.

Nice training they give these twassicks.

These people are so overzealous and out of touch that a lady who charges £200 an hour, would be deemed by HMRC to earn £4,800 a day!!! (See what I did there?) Then they just times that by seven days a week, 52 weeks a year. And the tax bill is therefore surmised to be on earnings of: 1, 747.200!!

You really could not make it up (but THEY do).

In the delusional grey matter of the institutionalised bean counter/investigative officer, sex workers are obviously drugged to gills and never sleep.

This is because primarily the media portrays prostitution in this manner, and, they most annoyingly ALWAYS have headlines which are trotted out with monotonous regularity, along the lines of: 'SHOULD PROSTITUTION BE LEGALISED?'

Misinformation and disinformation, propaganda and scare mongering are the tools of the state.

Were HMRC to have actually won the case, they would have made sure that the result would feature in every broadsheet they had in their pocket.

But, they didn't, and went away VERY quietly.

Hmmmmmm.

Post trial, there were a few national papers (supposedly) 'interested' in my case...but, even though they were approached by a journalist with whom they had previously enjoyed a close relationship, on reading the article…the subject matter was deemed by all the Editors as being: 'TOO CONTROVERSIAL'.

Which means (let us face it), the government controls what you can or cannot read.

God forbid that they should do an in depth investigative piece of stellar journalism with regard to Tax and Tarts, even for the most prurient of interest.

COOL DOWN

A scene in the sublime movie: 'Shawshank Redemption' resonates with me to this day.

Brooks, the old timer, having been incarcerated by the brutal regime at Shawshank, is suddenly released.

He found 'freedom' difficult, and, as we, the viewer, watch him prepare a hang mans' noose, in order to commit suicide, the movie voice over of his character states: 'I'M TIRED OF BEING AFRAID ALL THE TIME'.

Well, frankly my dears, so am I.............

THE END

TOO MANY COCKS SPOIL THE BROTHEL

A wonderful website devoted to the 'monumental shambles' which is HMRC: www.hmrcisshite.com, posted this story a few days ago....

'As has been reported some time ago HMRC make use of the internet and social networking sites to help identify possible tax evasion. Shout99 notes that even Google Street View is being used by HMRC to identify lifestyles beyond those which equate to the income reported by suspected tax evaders.

However, Street View is not "real time" and what it shows may be misinterpreted. UHY Hacker Young pointed to an example of a taxpayer being wrongly identified as sending his/her children to a private school, because of a Street View image showing his fence with a poster advertising the school's fete. It transpired that the poster was in fact on the neighbour's fence'.

As Littlejohn would say: 'YOU COULDN'T MAKE IT UP'...........

Printed in Great Britain
by Amazon.co.uk, Ltd.,
Marston Gate.